A Guide to Pare

Addressing Adolescence

Dr. Muhammad Abdul Bari

Ta-Ha Publishers Ltd.

© 1418 AH/1998 CE Ta-Ha Publishers Ltd.
First Published as 'The Greatest Gift: A Guide to Parenting from an Islamic Perspective' in Rabi al-Awwal 1419 AH/July 1998 CE
Revised and published as this edition 1432 AH/May 2011

Ta-Ha Publishers Ltd,
Unit 4, The Windsor Centre,
Windsor Grove, West Norwood,
London, SE27 9NT
UK

Website: **www.taha.co.uk**
E-mail: sales@taha.co.uk

Written by: **Dr. Muhammad Abdul Bari**
General Editor: **Dr. Abia Afsar-Siddiqui**
Book / Cover Design and Typeset by: **Shakir Abdulcadir .: open**squares**.co.uk**

A catalogue record of this book is available from the British Library
ISBN-13: 978 1 84200 125 7

Printed and bound by: **IMAK Ofset, Turkey**

**To my late parents
who showed me the way for a meaningful life.
May Allah bless their souls.**

Acknowledgements

This book is the outcome of my long-term involvement with youth and community work in Britain. Many people, including the very young and old, have contributed to the ideas contained in it. They all deserve my sincere thanks. The decision to write a book on parenting was further enhanced when I came across a respected elder who 'lost' his daughter. I was not sure how to console him at that time. I pray to Allah that no one faces that situation with their children. The pressure within me to start writing became stronger when I was approached by *Witness Pioneer* network, an internet based virtual organisation, to run a course on some social issues for their virtual school. I made up my mind to run the 'Islamic Perspective of Parenting' course. I am indebted to them for giving me the opportunity to run it through which I learnt a lot. I am also grateful to Dr. Jamil Sharif of Webstar Plc., London, who decided to run the same course on their *Salaam* web page with additional on-line question and answer facilities. In the same way, my participation in a week-long Facilitator Course on 'Strengthening Families and Strengthening Communities: An Inclusive Parent Programme' by the Race Equality Foundation (REF) in London was useful.

I express my deep appreciation of my wife, Sayeda, for her understanding, support and contribution in writing the book. In spite of the pressures of life, her excellent family management and sense of humour continuously encouraged me to sit at the computer. I am grateful to our four children, Rima, Raiyan, Labib and Adib for their enthusiasm during the process of writing. I am also indebted to a number of *ulema* in London for helping me find references from the Qur'an and *Hadith* books. May Allah shower His blessings on all of them.

Contents

Preface

When the son of Adam dies his actions are cut off except for three: a continuing sadaqah or charity, useful knowledge from which benefit is derived and a right-acting child who makes supplication for him. (Muslim and Ahmad)

At every stage in history, in every society and in every culture, there has been a generation 'gap' between parents and children, which seems to widen during the teenage years. The challenge for parents has always been to create good, well-rounded, happy citizens of the future and the success of this depends on how well children have been parented. Societies that have taken seriously the enormity of this responsibility have fared far better than those who dismiss or are too simplistic in their attitude towards parenting.

The transition from childhood into adolescence is generally not a smooth one. Children grow rapidly and experience physical changes in their body shape. Perhaps for the first time, they become more aware of themselves, their body and their personality. They become physically stronger, more imaginative and socially conscious, with sexual thoughts occupying their minds for a disproportionate amount of time. They want to look attractive, especially for the opposite sex. They become sensitive to comments and feel embarrassed by their own shortcomings. While dealing with this internal conflict, they are bombarded with the huge amount of information and 'messages' that surround us all. As adults, we have learnt to filter these but young people have to negotiate through the allure of permissive, amoral surroundings while emerging as dignified, noble young people, who are confident and comfortable within themselves and with their role in society.

This period of emergence as a young adult into the world may bring with it a spectrum of behaviour from moodiness to truancy, lack of respect for authority, anti-social behaviour, sexual promiscuity, teenage pregnancy, drug addiction and crime. The more permissive the surrounding society is, the further the boundaries are pushed and all of the above social issues become a very real concern. This can happen when, instead of religious or age-old moral and ethical values, base desires dictate human life, consumerism sets social agenda and society fears to set boundaries on behaviour. Ironically, in societies where freedom is over-restricted and young people are at the receiving end of continuous diktats from adults, social problems become an issue as many adolescents rebel against their constraining authority at the first opportunity. For young people to grow into good citizens and human beings, they need to be part of a society where freedom and responsibility are balanced.

Dealing with adolescents is not easy. Parents often feel that with the coming of the teenage years, the physical responsibility of parenting has diminished. But this is replaced with a more challenging parental role. Parents must now, more than ever, be not only mothers and fathers but most effective educators, guides, role models and friends to their sons and daughters. Building a deep and matured relationship on the basis of love, respect and loyalty with our children is vital for the well-being of the future generation.

In any case, while the parenting of an adolescent is a challenging but rewarding enterprise, for Muslims the parental obligation has an added dimension. Not only do Muslim parents need to provide their children with physical, emotional and intellectual nourishment, but equally importantly we also need to pass on Islamic beliefs and values thus providing them with spiritual nourishment as well. In order for Muslim parenting to be successful, it has to be dynamic and creative, forward looking and flexible, assertive and rational.

Islam's approach to life is holistic. With its transcendental value-system and clear focus of life, Islam has a unique way of preparing the younger generation of human beings for their future role. The *hadith* that: "No parent can give their child a better gift than good manners, good character and a good education"[1] puts a heavy burden on Muslim parents to invest in their children. Invest wisely, and the rewards are high. One only has to look back at the golden periods of Islamic history to see what heights can be attained when human potential is unleashed. Equally, history can provide plenty of examples of the depths to which human beings can plummet. It may be argued that the Muslim *ummah* is in just such a trough at the present time and this can be in part attributed to the lack of genuine attention to parenting skills.

However, it is time for us to rediscover and reclaim the spirit of Islam. Turning challenges into opportunities is part of the human spirit. Parenting adolescent children can be joyful, enterprising and adventurous if parents give importance to their job of parenting and look upon this as a part of life's learning curve.

Numerous books are available on this subject, but books written from a Muslim perspective are very few indeed. If we Muslims are serious about safeguarding our Muslim identity in a pluralist environment, building our families and community and working for the common good of all in society, assertive parenting is vital for the community agenda. Conscientious members of the Muslim community should thus

---

1 At-Tirmidhi

endeavour to work with others, Muslims and non-Muslims, and start a broader movement of 'positive parenting' before it is too late. The starting point for this is ensuring that the Muslim home environment is stable, caring and reassuring and also that the community is united in its effort to move forward.

Addressing Adolescence is my humble contribution to those Muslim parents who realise that parenting is a mission to recreate a new generation of human beings in the model of the righteous predecessors of Islam; a weighty trust for which we will be held accountable on the Day of Judgement.

The nature of the book is reader-friendly, not academic or scholarly. The principle followed is holistic and preventative, rather than piecemeal and curative. Human life is complex and as such there are many approaches when addressing an issue, depending on cultural or other variations. I have followed the broad Islamic principle, that is, anything not forbidden in Islam is acceptable. The book is about facing or addressing the challenges of parenting from an Islamic perspective. It is not meant to be a book of 'Parenting in Islam' nor a book of *fiqh*.

This book is primarily written for Muslims who are in minority situations, mainly in the West.[2] This should not, I think, jeopardise the common appeal of the book and I hope that any reader can benefit from it. The attempt to criticise the post-modern West has been done in context and as objectively as possible. In the same manner, the Muslim world and the East have also been criticised. The purpose is to put forward the best of the two. I apologise if I have failed in that objectivity.

---

2 It is accepted that the word 'West' is not limited to geographical boundary. In referring to the West, the European, North American and Australasian countries are included. However, due to globalisation in recent decades the discussion on East or West has essentially become pedantic as more Muslims permanently live in Europe, America and Australia than many Muslim countries. Similarly, many indigenous Westerners also now live in the East and/or Muslim countries.

My passion in writing this book is to create more awareness in as many Muslim parents as possible and take them through the complex but essential journey of parenting in this unpredictable social milieu. It is an attempt to regenerate the Muslim communities of the West through 'common sense' parenting. This is a 'parent to parent' book, not an 'expert to layperson' one. My credential is my continuous work in the grass-root Muslim communities and fervent desire to be a better parent by facilitating numerous parenting courses over the years. I rely on the forgiveness of Allah for my shortcomings and pray that He accepts this humble work.

Chapter One

The Challenges of Adolescence

Allah has called them the 'dutiful' (al-Abrar) because they are dutiful (birr) to their parents and children. Just as you have a duty which you owe your parent, so you have a duty which you owe your child. (Al-Adab al-Mufrad al-Bukhari)

A Nightmare or Knightly Power?

Adolescence has always attracted criticism from elders for its restlessness and its rash and impulsive outbursts. On the positive side, it draws attention for its creative enterprise, vitality and enthusiasm. It is the period when human beings discover their energy and potential and aspire to do something adventurous and unique. If driven by high spiritual, social and moral values and positive social norms, its creative and dynamic power can lift a nation to great heights, but misguided adolescence is a destructive force that can let a society down and create havoc.

During the first few generations of Islam, and in other cyclical moments of expansion and renewal, some adolescents or post-adolescents even took the lead in enduring great sacrifice and expanding the frontiers of Islam with their humanity, zeal and vigour. Most notable among these was Muhammad bin Qasim, who rose to the peak of fame for his chivalry and spirituality in his late teens, as a leader in the Umayyad period. When the Muslim *ummah* became too complacent with its past glory, the energy of youth was misused in vain pursuits and periods of retreat and decline ensued.

The direction in which young people expend their youthful energy is very strongly governed by the path along which their parents and close ones steer them. It is imperative therefore, that parents have a strong understanding of the issues relevant to their adolescent; equip their child with the resources to become a good Muslim adult for the benefit of society as a whole, adopting a method that is neither too liberal nor too authoritarian.

The Great Change

Young children normally mirror what their parents have taught them and conform relatively easily to their parents' wishes. The adolescent, however, is a completely different self. As children cross the threshold from childhood and begin their exciting trek into young adulthood, they undergo extraordinary changes in their bodies as well as in their feelings and emotions. Growing up is a once-in-a-lifetime experience, exhilarating for some and painful and very complex for others. Either way, adjusting to this sudden change in life is not easy.

With the emergence of a new adult, comes a new personality. This can swing from charming and wonderful to moody and insolent. It is at this stage that parents must learn to change their own attitudes towards their offspring and consider them as individuals in their own right. Their distinctive features should not only be tolerated, but wholeheartedly embraced. The parenting skills employed in the rearing of young children will now be tested and many parents feel stretched and stressed with their 'new' children. Some parents adopt a lax attitude and leave their adolescents to grow without boundaries, while rigid and dominating parents impose too many constraints. Neither of these attitudes is healthy. Conscientious parents, however, adjust quickly to the reality that an unpredictable change in their children's behaviour is on the way and engage with their children in a reassuring manner, with patience and understanding.

It is difficult to pinpoint with accuracy when exactly adolescence starts. It can start at the age of ten, sixteen or even eighteen, but generally, it spans the teenage period. So, what happens at this stage? What is the myth and what is the reality surrounding adolescence?

Adolescence is the beginning of the end of childhood and thrusts young people into the world of responsibility. As it is a time of internal commotion in young people's lives, parents need to observe them closely and guide them through this period of need. The changes that children undergo are physical, emotional, social, intellectual and spiritual.

Physical

The physical change, known as puberty, activates the body clock of children to function in a different mode and prepares them to be physically capable of reproduction. In girls, the production of increasing amounts of the female sex hormone, oestrogen, brings about a more feminine body shape and the onset of menstruation. Boys grow more rapidly than girls in height and weight with increasing amounts of testosterone in their body. Additionally, masculine characteristics such as the breaking of the voice and body hair are established. Energetic as they are, adolescent boys and girls need more nutrition for their growth, intellectual nourishment for their minds and spiritual nourishment for their self-control.

Parents should not only be aware of these changes in their children, but should acquire the basic tools to deal with them. As puberty descends upon children, mothers and fathers need to open discussions with their daughters and sons respectively, as frankly and decently as possible, about important issues regarding puberty and adult life. These include cleanliness after menstruation and wet dreams, the removal of unwanted body hair and the *fiqh* (jurisprudence) regarding basic Islamic rites. While sensitivity is the guiding principle, embarrassment should not prevent parents teaching their children the necessities of adult life. The Qur'an itself discusses sensitive issues in a decent manner. It should not be considered taboo to discuss sex and sexuality. Indeed, if this is not done in a decent manner within an Islamic context then children will most probably learn incorrect information from elsewhere and perhaps in an unpalatable way. Needless to say, that a healthy and deep parent-child relationship is the essential foundation for successful dialogue and discussion about this subject.

Puberty is also the period from when the *Shari'ah* is enforceable on a Muslim. In other words, according to Islam, boys and girls are considered to be responsible men and women, even though they may still be teenagers. The core of a healthy, moral society should be a dignified relationship between men and women that does not overstep the bounds of decency. Islamic rulings are detailed and exacting about the extent and nature of relationships between members of the opposite gender. In Surah an-Nisa, verse 23, there is a list of people that are *mahrams*, in other words, people that one cannot marry. When Muslims (including pubescent boys and girls) find themselves in the company of non-*mahrams*, they should be aware of their conduct and dress code and maintain conscious awareness of the presence and knowledge of Allah whenever they encounter one another in public places.

Emotional

Physical development brings natural shyness and embarrassment in adolescents. These and other emotional changes come as a result of the hormonal disruptions in their bodies and from their growing responsibilities. Because adolescents do not have any control over their physical growth, this enforced change can create feelings of confusion in them. As they are perceived differently by people around them, the ensuing psychological and emotional changes can make them unreasonable and unpredictable. They themselves cannot decide whether they are still children or adults and do not know in which category they fit or belong to. It can take a while to sort through these feelings. Sensitive parents and the adults around them do not press too hard on their adolescents to fit into the adult world. Rather, they give them space and time to settle on their own.

Social

Young adults know that they are still dependant on their parents but are aware that they must become self-reliant and assert their independence. They do this in ways that may seem disruptive to household routines and to push the boundaries that parents may have previously set. For example, adolescents may resent participating in family activities, be discourteous to younger siblings and rude to elders. They may be interested in reading more adult books or magazines, listening to music and watching TV programmes which parents may disapprove of. They may sometimes come home late and refuse to go shopping with their parents or visit family friends. They may insist their parents buy them certain expensive designer clothes or games.

Understandably, some parents will feel that this behaviour is not acceptable, but children are under a great deal of pressure to conform to the youth culture of wider society that they see through their peers' actions and through the media. The degree of success in dealing with this behaviour depends on the parent-child relationship, personality of the parents and how much quality time they can spend with their adolescent children. The best way is the middle way: neither dictatorial nor permissive. Parents are neither equals nor bosses, but should aim to be their children's best confidants. A right balance and sense of proportion, though difficult to maintain, are the way forward. Parents need to train, guide and explain to their children what their boundaries are, what Islam requires of them and why. Children should neither feel that they are being ignored, nor should they be able to get away with unacceptable behaviour. Once they understand the dynamics of the family and community and their role within these, then they will gradually learn to be responsible social human beings and take their place in the community and in the wider society.

The Issues

The various changes during the adolescent period bring new challenges, worries and threats that can alter family relationships. Sensitive parents quickly learn to adjust and accommodate, and they adopt a different strategy to deal with the situation and harness the youthful energy of their adolescents. In order to do this, we need to be aware of what our children are going through in order to best communicate with them in a timely manner.

Sex

Puberty brings with it a heightened interest in members of the opposite sex. This is a time when passions and emotions run high. It is all too tempting for young people to give in to their whims and desires at this stage especially when society around them considers it the norm to have boyfriends and girlfriends and engage in a sexual relationship. Uncontrolled mixing of the sexes and the resultant over-indulgence are so commonplace that segregation or separation of sexes is considered backward and oppressive. Yet indulging in casual relationships at this age has negative emotional and physical effects on the young people involved as well as creating problems in society. Many developed countries are facing a significant issue with unwanted teenage pregnancy and all the negative consequences of this.

In societies based on good moral and spiritual standards, young people's energies are spent on creative and meaningful pursuits. Islam has specific etiquettes (*adab*) for interaction between men and women. Muslim men and women are asked to be modest in their appearance, lower their gaze, dress appropriately and avoid physical proximity with the opposite sex (Surah an-Nur 24:30-31). The *Shari'ah* provides young Muslim men and women the opportunity to develop their full potential and marry as soon as possible to start families and, most importantly, to channel their sex-drives for the pleasure of Allah. This is important for retaining purity of character and in order to achieve this, deep faith, self-discipline, good company and strong family anchorage are vital.

Hijab and Modesty

In a world where the provocative display of women's bodies is portrayed as glamorous and progressive, the *hijab*, of course, looks odd. As a result, some people take this modest dress as a symbol of oppression. To them, the *hijab* is a barrier that imprisons women and keeps them subservient in a man's world.

Why is the *hijab* so important in Islam? The answer to this is simple. The command concerning the *hijab* is from Allah, the Almighty, Who alone knows where the dignity of human beings lies. There are excellent reasons behind His commands and they are for the benefit of all humans. Women are blessed with physical beauty and a soft and gentle nature in contrast to the more sexually aggressive nature of man. The *hijab* works to protect women from the possible lewd thoughts and glances of men as well as protecting men from being taken in by a woman's beauty. The *hijab* gives dignity to every individual woman to be respected as a human being for her talents and character rather than her looks.

This reflects the high position that women enjoy in Islam. As a human being she is an emissary of Allah on earth, as a daughter she is a blessing for her father, as a wife she is half the *deen* of her husband and as a mother she has the highest position for her children, their Paradise under her feet. In Islam, the role of men and women complement each other for the greater good of society, but individually each person is accountable to Allah on his or her own merit. The fact that some Muslim societies marginalise their women has nothing to do with Islam, but to do with ignorance and decadence in all aspects of their lives. Sadly for them, cultural baggage sometimes takes precedence over Islamic guidelines.

Dress, of course, is an essential ingredient of the *hijab*, but the spirit and attitude behind it are fundamentally important. Merely putting on a piece of cloth to cover one's body and hair is not the same as adopting the *hijab*. When the external symbol of purity and modesty marry with internal submission to the will of Allah, the *hijab* elevates women to social and spiritual heights. Here are a few comments from those who have experienced the pleasure of the *hijab*.

> The *hijab* is the most wonderful dress for women in the world. It gives women a sense of security in the world of prying eyes. (A young Muslim convert)

> Many non-Muslim women might think of such a dress as restrictive or even oppressive, a sign of submission to men. But those who have adopted the *hijab* find it nothing less than liberating. (A Muslim convert)

It's the total opposite of subordination. We wear it because we choose to; we refuse to let ourselves be sex objects. We're saying: "Value us for what we are, our character, not how we look. We're not going to play the game of trying to look good for you. We won't let you hire us because you like our legs, or we'll look good around the office." (A Muslim scholar)

The religious mandate of modest dress is hardly limited to Islam. Observant Jewish women, for example, are urged to cover their hair and bodies to hide their beauty in public. Nun's habits are rooted in a religious call for modesty, as well. (A Muslim activist)

The following is an excerpt from a poem that gives an insight about the debate on *hijab*.

Object of Despair[3]

Emma (a typical post-modern girl):
"You are a smart girl Ayesha,
Why do you wear that across your hair?
Subjugated by 'man'kind
An object of despair.

Take it off my sister
Let your banner be unfurled.
Don't blindly follow all around
DECLARE YOUR FREEDOM TO THE WORLD."

---

3 *Abu Omar, Courtesy of Witness-Pioneer*

Ayesha (a conscientious Muslim girl):

"My dear sister Emma,
Why do you dress the way you do?
The skirt you're wearing round your waist
Is it really you?

Now that we've sat down
I see you tug it across your thighs,
Do you feel ashamed?
Aware of prying eyes?

In the main, its men my friend
Who dictate the whims of fashion,
Generating all the garb
To incite the base's passion.

Be free my sister Emma
Escape from your deep mire,
Don *hijab* today my friend
And all Islam's attire.

To use your very words my friend
Let your banner be unfurled.
Don't blindly follow all around
DECLARE YOUR FREEDOM TO THE WORLD."

Undoubtedly, it is a challenge for young Muslim girls to don the *hijab* when social pressure on them to imitate so-called 'mainstream' culture is enormous. It is natural for humans to give emphasis to looks and especially at a time when girls may want to appear attractive to boys, they may experiment with heavy make-up, wear revealing or tight clothes and style their hair in unnatural ways. This can be a way of rebelling against parental authority or simply following the current social trend. After all, it is easier to be carried along with the currents like froth on water, but it requires strength to swim against the flow.

It is important at this point for parents (particularly mothers through their own example) to teach their daughters the importance of the *hijab* as a part of maintaining purity of character and dignity of personality, a means for their empowerment and their identity as a Muslim. Girls who adopt *hijab* may be treated in a negative manner by people who do not understand their choice. Here, parental support and the company of other good friends will make the difference between a girl who continues to maintain her *hijab* for the pleasure of Allah and one who may cave into pressure to take it off.

Beard

Keeping a beard is the Prophetic tradition or *sunnah* and is recommended for adult Muslim men. Prophet Muhammad ﷺ said, "Trim closely the moustache and grow the beard" (Sahih Muslim). The beard is a mark of masculinity and in the past was seen as a symbol of authority in some cultures where leaders and powerful men kept a beard. In modern times, however, it is seen as more attractive to be clean-shaven or to keep a small amount of facial hair out of fashion.

The fact remains that the best of all men, the Prophets of Allah, kept a beard and Prophet Muhammad ﷺ recommended that the men among his followers do the same. Therefore, it is important for parents (particularly fathers through their own example) to show proper respect to this important *sunnah* of the Prophet ﷺ.

Friendship and Company

Good company is an essential ingredient for maintaining sound character in youth, especially in permissive societies, and friendship should be taken seriously by Muslims (Surah al-Furqan 25:27-30).

A group of moral and pious young people will protect each other from social diseases and encourage each other to do good. Being part of a like-minded group is a source of emotional support as well as giving people confidence to lead their lives positively in the midst of everyday challenges. However, finding genuine friends is not always easy. Parents should keep an eye on those their adolescents hang around and lend their support in finding suitable friends, if needed. This does not necessarily mean that children should have friends from the same faith, ethnic or linguistic origin only. Islam transcends the boundaries of race and language. What is important is the good moral character of the friend.

There is an erroneous view in some Muslim quarters that Muslims should not have non-Muslim friends, arguing that the Qur'an states that non-believers should not be taken as *'awliya'* (Surah Ali Imran 3:28). Every human being has different types of friendship, from the closest bosom friends to good, casual friends through to acquaintances and colleagues. Bosom friends or confidants are those with whom people share intimate aspects of their life and they are normally of the same nature, culture or religion.

Everyone needs trusted friends. Conversely, undesirable friends or bad company can ruin an adolescent's life, as young people tend to conform to peer pressure, the surrounding youth culture and dominant social trends. Some children, especially in upper school, feel pressured into playing truant from school, 'hanging around' with their 'mates' in shopping malls or local parks during school time and sometimes indulging in anti-social behaviour. It is imperative that parents work with schools to resolve this problem early if they have good reason to believe that their children are doing this. Parents need to be assertive with their adolescents in keeping them away from undesirable company.

Aside from maintaining a social interaction with all, male and female, Muslim boys and girls should avoid getting closer to people of the opposite gender. There is no concept in Islam of having 'mates' from the opposite sex. When they meet in public places they need to observe Islamic etiquettes. The reason for this apparently rigid guideline is to close the doors to something that is unacceptable and *haram*, that is, meeting or spending time in seclusion (*khalwa*) with someone who is a non-*mahram* and gradually being drawn into an extra-marital sexual relationship. However, modest interaction in a mixed environment for necessary social and educational reasons in a public place is fine.

School and Career

By the time children have entered adolescence they are most probably already in secondary school. This is the start of their future career. The decision of which school to choose has always been a dilemma for parents and a later chapter has been dedicated to looking at this subject in more detail.

In short, parents should look for the best school that they can afford. A good well-resourced Islamic school is of course a priority for many Muslim parents, if that is available and affordable. Parents should avoid schools that do not have enough credibility in terms of educational standards and discipline, and their tackling of bullying, racism and Islamophobia. Children with special needs, whether they are gifted or underachievers for cognitive or physical reasons, should have their needs met with specialist provision by qualified persons.

The chosen school should be well placed to encourage and guide children towards careers in which they succeed and thrive. Some parents, for whatever reason, may not be able to help their children and this is where the school's input becomes more important.

The career decisions that a young person makes affect them for the rest of their life. In making such decisions, young Muslims should not only seek material success and status in life, they should be encouraged to choose a career that will help them earn a *halal* income from honest hard work. Giving something back to the community, being of some benefit to society and working for a successful Hereafter should be priorities. Muslims are forbidden to be involved in any job or business that is *haram* or that promotes *haram*, including alcohol, drugs, pornography, interest – whether as a long-term career decision or a short-term weekend or holiday job. It is equally *haram* to make money through dishonesty, gambling, fraud, exploitation and interest on savings. Prophet Muhammad ﷺ did not fear about poverty for his *ummah* but feared about worldly riches and so it is important that the youth of our *ummah* are not driven by greed and corrupted by mere material considerations. Equally, young people should never think of depending on social welfare and benefit systems and should refrain from taking benefits unless absolutely necessary. Earning, saving, investing and spending in a *halal* way are vital for leading a Muslim life.

Money Matters

With increasing levels of independence, the question of money soon arises. Should adolescents earn money for themselves? At what age? Should they contribute to their living expenses? These are questions that can only be answered by each family for themselves, keeping in mind their financial condition.

A genuinely needy family has no recourse but to involve an adolescent in earning for their minimum sustenance. In fact, it is a duty to help the family keep up a decent living standard. But, whatever the situation, adolescents should not be denied their right to an education, both worldly and religious. There are 'penny wise, pound foolish' parents who spoil the careers of their children in pursuit of earning immediate money and in the process destroy their children's lives and the community's future.

However, adolescents are young adults and as such, should know the importance of money and how to handle it. It may be that a part-time weekend or holiday job may prove useful in giving young people a sense of responsibility and financial acumen. However, this must not hamper their education or compromise their *deen* in any way.

Personal Flaws to Watch Out For

As children enter adolescence, they prefer to spend less time with their parents and more on their own in front of the TV, computer, mobile or with their peer group. In the absence of any sensitive mentoring and guidelines from parents or responsible adults, they are likely to be heavily influenced by the prevalent culture. Some of the permissive ideas and practices that are commonplace in modern society are not compatible with an Islamic lifestyle. Parents who ignore, procrastinate or fail to assert in guiding their young ones at this stage may find themselves dealing with one or more of the following problems:

Egocentrism

Children may acquire two opposing characteristics in adolescence; one outward looking and the other inward looking. Embarrassment because of their changing bodies and other factors can take over and cause them to develop an individualistic and self-centred attitude. Under the powerful influences of TV, computer-games and other technological gadgets, they may find excuses to withdraw from the family and social affairs. A young person who does not have any siblings or close friendships may find themselves feeling alone. Parental incompetence or indifference can exacerbate this problem. If children fail to relate to the family, the community and wider society, all sorts of psychological inadequacies can find a home in them and give rise to inappropriate personal habits and social ills.

Rudeness and Bad Manners

A Persian mystic said long ago, "What a dichotomy, the softest part of our body can inflict the hardest pain!" He was, of course, talking about the power of the tongue.

Rude words and bad language can cause much anguish escalating into fights and disharmony between family members. Children must be trained in how to control their tongues. It is better to maintain silence than to say something inappropriate or bad that may later be a cause of regret. The balanced development of a human being is enhanced in a sound environment of love and compassion and with smiles and good words. On the other hand, children can grow to be unpleasant and hurtful adults in an unhealthy environment of rudeness, ill manners, anger and frustration. Parents who practice gentleness in their speech with each other and with their children and avoid rudeness, even under provocation, reap the benefit of similar mannerisms in their offspring. If rudeness and ill manners do arise in children then they need to be dealt with promptly and strongly, but with sensitivity. There is never any cause to be rude or disrespectful to children, even when disciplining or sanctioning them.

Distasteful Styles and Fashions

It is becoming more and more a social trend to blindly follow often distasteful and improper styles and fashions. What is the reason for this craze?

Self-esteem and a sense of self-worth are vital to the well-being of every person and are what motivate people and give meaning to their lives. Some people tend to achieve these through external manifestations such as provocative clothing, body piercing, tattoos and dramatic hairstyles. Others wish to make a statement, gain a sense of identity or attract attention through these means.

For believers (the *muminun)*, self-appreciation, sense of identity and meaning of life all come from their faith, their knowledge of Allah and striving to please Him. Islam has given a dress code and a code of morals and conduct that beautify a Muslim's life. By following these, a Muslim can feel content and satisfied from within and conduct their life with dignity and nobility.

Young people often do not realise that the 'feel good' factor of following distasteful fashions or trying to attract the attention of the opposite sex through the way they dress is transient and at the expense of decency and dignity. None of this bothers high earners in the fashion industry, but it should be a cause for concern to caring Muslim parents.

Lying and Cheating

People lie because they fear that the truth will bring negative consequences. However, the world through a child's eyes is different. They may imagine, dream, visualise or fantasise about something and tell others. As adolescents are going through a transition period, they may develop the tendency to conceal, lie or cheat and there may be a number of reasons for this:

» To make fun, play with others or manipulate, confuse or control;
» To present a better image of themselves;
» To extract something from their parents or get their attention;
» To get out of trouble or avoid someone's anger;
» To avoid facing an unpleasant truth;
» To maintain a fantasy they have developed.

They may resort to cheating in order to:

» Maintain self-esteem through success, as they cannot accept failure;
» Avoid the consequences of their behaviour;
» Make themselves acceptable to others;
» Get a better reward.

All these should be taken into consideration when tackling the problem and parents should examine whether it is their own behaviour that may be fuelling the problem. In open, transparent and healthy family environments, there is no place for lying or cheating as many of the reasons for lying have been pre-empted. Lying needs to be dealt with promptly and children must be taught that this is a serious human defect. It is a grave wrong action in Islam, as it is known as the 'mother of all wrong actions' and is the strongest sign of *nifaq* (hypocrisy).

> *The signs of a hypocrite are three - when speaks he tells a lie, when he promises he breaks it and when he is entrusted with anything he deceives.* (Sahih al-Bukhari)

Disobedience and Rebellion

Very often teenagers cannot articulate their reasons for anger and frustration or feel that they are not being listened to when they try to talk. The resulting swirl of emotion within them manifests itself as rebellious behaviour and disobedience. It is understandable that parents become stressful when their children display severe behavioural problems. But it is very important we become more reflective when this happens. What are the triggers and context for this behaviour? Is the current home environment or parental behaviour in some way contributing to the problem? What can parents do to try to stop this behaviour?

However bad the behaviour, we must rise above it and remember that Allah, the Almighty, keeps on tolerating the worst wrongdoers on earth and continues to provide generously for them. Whatever the offence, children should not be dealt with so harshly that the relationship is severed or they feel compelled to rebel. Parents should have the basic qualities of patience, anger management and stress control and should always try to maintain dialogue and open communication with their children.

Mental Health and Self-Harm

Self-harm is a widespread problem in many societies. According to The Mental Health Foundation, nearly 1 in 15 people between the ages of 11 and 25 deliberately hurt themselves.[4] This is a disturbing phenomenon and although there has been some research on this, it is still a largely misunderstood area. Survival instinct and inner resilience are embedded in human nature. There are a number of factors, psychological and socio-economic, that determine why and how some people do not consider their life worth living and resort to self-harm:

» Undergoing difficult experiences in childhood or adolescence such as physical violence and emotional or sexual abuse;

» Neglect;

» Separation from loved ones;

» Bullying, harassment, assault;

» Isolation.

There are various ways of self-harming or deliberately hurting or injuring oneself. The most common is cutting or burning and others include taking overdoses of medication, pulling out hair, scratching or tearing at skin causing sores, punching themselves, and throwing themselves against something. For some young people it is part of

---

4 Reported in London *Metro* on 27 March 2006

coping with a specific problem. A few people who self-harm may even go on to commit suicide. Experts define self-harm by other names, such as, deliberate self-harm, attempted suicide, para-suicide, self-mutilation and self-injury.

If children do not receive proper support and legitimate emotional outlets during difficult times, they may lose their self-esteem, turn their anger or frustration inward, start blaming themselves and self-harm.

Whatever the reasons, self-harm goes against the spirit of Islam. Allah sends tests and trials throughout a person's life and promises rewards for the patient ones (Surah al-Baqarah 2:155-156). Patience comes from a deep belief and trust in Allah through knowledge and understanding of Islam that whatever He has decreed is for the best. If Muslim parents raise their children with love, care and understanding, then the issue of self-harm should not arise in their life, insha'Allah. Parents should educate their children in how to deal with difficult times and frustrations in addition to providing their support during such times.

Eating Disorders

An eating disorder is an abnormal relationship with food and obsession with weight that has an adverse effect on physical and mental health. There are two eating disorders: anorexia nervosa and bulimia. Anorexia nervosa is a condition in which a person starves themselves in order to be thin. They believe that if they eat or even drink anything they will get fat, so they control their diet to an extreme degree. Sufferers of anorexia have an emaciated, unnaturally thin look.

In the case of bulimia, the person craves food and wants to eat but believes that food will make them fat. So they will binge eat (overeat) and then either make themselves sick or misuse laxatives in order to purge themselves. Sufferers may not appear to have a weight problem but their weight may fluctuate. Anorexia can start in the mid-teens and bulimia usually starts a little later. Both disorders are far more common in girls than in boys.

The reasons for eating disorders are complex and not fully understood. The idea of becoming a woman may frighten a girl to such an extent that she starves herself in order to maintain a child-like body. It may simply be that society's image of an ideal woman is a slim one and in that quest for perfection, a young person may go too far. The problem is not just a physical one but also a psychological one. It is difficult for a parent to understand why their anorexic child cannot just pick up a piece of food and eat it, but that child genuinely believes that they are fat and that eating food will cause them to lose control. Parents can start by having a healthy attitude towards food in the home by encouraging a balanced diet for the whole family which includes the moderate consumption of anything that is *halal* and nutritious. It is also not a good idea to make disparaging comments about anyone's weight, especially during the sensitive time of puberty. If the family can all eat at least one meal a day together, it becomes easier for any eating problems to become apparent early on and to be dealt with promptly by a professional.

How to Deal with Difficult Issues

As boys and girls grow in their distinctive ways, fathers and mothers respectively, should make sure their children can comfortably:

» Adjust themselves as individual men and women;
» Conform with their family and with the people close to them;
» Find their position among others in the wider world.

Not every child grows in the same way. Some pass through their adolescence peacefully and smoothly, others have a turbulent time. Young people in their mid-teens can present a battlefield to their parents in a number of areas, such as untidiness, unpredictable moods, depression, lack of concentration, lethargy and staying out late. A stable family environment, an Islamic ethos at home and in the community, good and reliable friends and high expectations and praise from parents and teachers are ingredients for winning this battle. It is tempting for parents in a liberal and permissive society to become over-protective. However, if parents do not give children enough space and freedom within the bounds of Islam, the results are almost always negative. The following tried and tested suggestions are useful during the adolescent years.

Show Extra Sympathy and Empathy

Children are under all sorts of pressure nowadays. Boys and girls are expected to follow the trends, admire celebrity role models and conform to the new wave of youth culture. These have an impact on their dress, appearance and manners. Faced with this situation, young people need someone to empathise with them and parents are best placed to do this. We need to understand what goes on in our children's world and positively, though not intrusively, show an interest in their wellbeing. Children need guidance and help from someone close to them in looking after their health, watching their friendships and guiding them in life.

Even though it may not be easy to feel affection for a continually badly behaved child, it is at this stage of life that they will most need sympathy. They will benefit from limitless unconditional love and knowing their broader boundaries. They will appreciate their parents spending quality time with them: talking, laughing, touching and hugging, all of which are important for a child's emotional needs.

Give Privacy and Personal Space

Adolescents suddenly become self-conscious especially about their body and self. They need privacy and, often, time on their own to reflect and to think. Ideally, they should be provided their own room, if parents can afford it. If not, brothers and sisters should at least be separated before the signs of adolescence. The level of space and privacy given depends on the age and intellectual maturity of the child. Parents do, however, need to know what goes on in their children's rooms and what is being kept there, and this should be found out with tact. Computers, landline telephones and TVs should be kept in communal areas for use by the whole family and not in individual bedrooms, where misuse may occur. It is also a good idea to negotiate limits on the usage of a mobile phone.

Accord Respect

A culture of respect within the family will give the foundation for young people to behave respectfully to everyone within the family and the wider society. Greeting with peace - *assalamualaikum* - showing respect to each other, such as knocking before entering someone's room, are all part and parcel of Islamic *adab*, especially from the period of adolescence. Parents need to discuss and practice the Prophetic examples on this. His ﷺ decent practices in the home were exemplary. On greeting his married daughter, Fatimah ﷺ later in life, he used to stand up and spread his garment for her.

Use Moderation

Moderation is the key to a successful parent-child relationship. Authoritarian parents make things worse for their children by trying to impose their opinions and will on them. Their patronising attitude kills off dynamism and creativity and creates simmering discontent, which at a later stage can give rise to rebellion. On the contrary, easy-going parents callously ignore their children by not intervening, even in times of necessity. They are either too liberal or are indifferent to their children and consider them adults when they are not. This leads young people to lose basic discipline in life. In an amoral post-modern society, this liberalism can be fatal for children.

Being 'tough and tender' or using a 'carrot and stick' policy is a sensible approach that educationalists and psychologists generally advocate nowadays in teaching children. Islam also embodies the 'middle way' as the best way of dealing with everything and the Prophet Muhammad ﷺ always adopted moderation. Parental success depends on firmness and fairness.

Ignore Sibling Arguments

Sibling rivalry is common in families where there are brothers and sisters of similar ages. It is a normal part of childhood development and is how siblings spend their time, enjoy and relax. They learn from each other through argument, loud talk and heated debate. They enrich the family by talking, laughing, complaining and even crying. This may be stressful for parents, but unless it is essential to intervene, parents should leave their children to sort things out between themselves. If it is necessary to get involved, then parents should never be biased or even appear to be so. Often the elder child gets the blame and the younger child gets the parents' sympathy. This should not automatically be the case. Elder children can be taught to be kind to their younger siblings while younger ones should be taught to respect their elder siblings. As with many issues, sibling rivalry phases out with time and, insha'Allah, matures into a healthy loving relationship.

Involve them in the Meaningful Pursuits of Life

It is through getting involved with meaningful pursuits, rather than giving in to shallow desires, that young people can truly achieve their potential in later life. There are now a variety of well-run reliable groups, clubs and associations in most major cities as well as organisations that promote community harmony and positive changes in society and service to others.

Muslim teenagers should be encouraged to become actively involved in civic responsibilities. Parents should help them in finding reliable groups with balanced social, moral and spiritual dimensions where they will thrive as practising and active Muslims. Unfortunately, there are groups that are bent on emotionalism or known to have only partial or one-sided views of Islam. Unwitting association with such groups can impede the development of character among young Muslims today. At all times, a balance must be maintained between participation in such groups, education, family responsibilities, Islamic activities and acts of service to others.

Provide Wholesome Recreation

Recreation is essential for the renewal of one's energy. Human beings cannot work like machines; we are capable of more than that. Our bodies and minds need relaxation in order to perform to their best. Finding relaxation through vain pursuits does nothing to further the mind and spirit: the use of intoxicants damages the body and sensual pleasures damage spirituality. Prophet Muhammad ﷺ recommended teaching young people horse riding, archery and swimming. Innocent games and exercises are a means for physical fitness and joy as well as sources of self-confidence and physical strength, all of which are vital for the well-being of the individual. Parents should pro-actively suggest activities that their children can get involved in. Too many do's and don'ts from parents often make children feel deprived and they may start to feel resentful towards their parents or even their religion.

Get them Involved in the Family

Muslim adolescents should gradually become responsible members of their families. Only then can they genuinely become part of the Muslim community and the wider society. The feeling of family loyalty and togetherness is also important for a lasting impact on the Muslim family ethos among children. Children should gradually be involved in the affairs of their families, starting with minor household chores. Regular family sessions create opportunities for free discussion of issues of interest, importance and concern which in turn create cohesion and homogeneity in the family. Adolescents should be encouraged to talk and speak their minds so that they feel confident and learn from everybody. Making their own contributions on a topic gives them a sense of responsibility and ownership. The early years of adult life are an indication of the person that they have the potential to become. As children grow, their playful mentality should be replaced by the mature and responsible pursuit of life and a sense of urgency to work for the *ummah* and beyond. Life is a serious business that needs a serious approach.

Manage your Anger

What if a serious crisis really occurs in a family with an adolescent? The most important thing to remember in that situation is to keep one's nerve and resort to a reasonable solution, even in extreme situations. We sometimes hear of fathers who resort to physical violence towards their daughters out of anger that they may have had an affair with someone outside their religion or culture.

Many parents think about their own dignity and family pride before basic Islamic demands. Some, out of love for their children or fear of being termed 'backward' by others, neglect their fundamental duty of giving their young ones Islamic nourishment. As a result, when their spiritually impoverished children stray away from their religion, parents suddenly wake up and try to harshly impose their decisions on them. But it is too late.

Human beings are not robots that can suddenly be programmed to behave with piety. Frustration and anger have never helped. They work like fire, igniting emotion and creating havoc. The Prophetic traditions on anger management are illuminating:

Anger is from the shaytan, and the shaytan is created from fire, and fire is extinguished by water. So, if one of you becomes angry let him perform wudu. (Abu Dawud)

If one of you becomes angry, let him be silent. (Ahmad)

If one of you becomes angry while he is standing, let him sit down, and if he is still angry let him lie down. (Ahmad)

What is needed is a level-headed and calm approach where the channels of communication are kept open. Like most things in life, there is no quick fix or immediate solution to any problem. Unfortunately, 'human beings are ever hasty' (Surah al-Isra 17:11).

Ask for Help

While it can be emotionally disturbing for parents to deal with 'difficult' children, the solution lies in preparation, understanding and effort. Children grow in the laps of their parents, so the symptom of any problem should be diagnosed well in time. If parents find it difficult to mould their children's characters in the colour of Islam they should consult friends, imams and experts, rather than giving up or procrastinating in the hope that one day they will come to their senses. Procrastination is the enemy. Only a knowledge-based, caring and timely intervention can bring a remedy in this situation.

There is no shame in asking other members of the community for help. There are many parents who may have been in similar positions and parents will find support and practical advice from these quarters. Also parents should bear in mind that supplication from the heart for their offspring can work miracles, by the will of Allah.

Chapter Two

The Onslaught of Social Ills

Evil enters like a needle and spreads like an oak tree.
(Ethiopian proverb)

The Proliferation of Sickness

It is sickness, not health, that spreads easily. Just as infectious diseases spread in congenial conditions, social ills also spread rapidly in a permissive environment. The pressure on individuals to confirm is very high indeed, and particularly so for young people. Adolescents generally lack stability and maturity. They are not yet prepared to face the challenges of life and have not yet grasped fully what life means to them.

Parents must have an awareness of the issues that affect their children in their lives and in the context of their surroundings, so that we can guide them and offer them a mature understanding of life that they lack. The following are a few major social problems relevant to young people in modern society.

Bullying and Intimidation

Bullying is a major and common problem, not only in schools but also in the work place. In an increasingly Islamophobic environment Muslim children may find this more of a problem. Bullying leaves long term psychological effects on the victims and destroys their confidence. Bullies themselves lack self-esteem, perhaps having experienced abuse in their lives, and thus transfer their anger and frustrations onto their victim. Anyone can become the target of a bully, but loners, socially passive people and those from minority groups may be more likely targets.

Parents should prepare their children to be assertive and instil confidence in them to face this challenge. They need to ensure that a trust is built with children during their early years so that they do not fail to inform an adult about bullying, if it ever occurs to them. In addition, Muslim children should be taught that all human beings are born innocent and that there is no room in Islam for bullying anyone (Surah al-Hujurat 49:11).

Anti-Social Behaviour (ASB)

Anti-social behaviour covers a whole range of selfish and unacceptable activities that have negative effects on people and can blight the quality of community life. ASB among children can arise as a result of a poor family environment with inattentive parenting, difficulties in schooling and educational attainment, failings in the community, mental illness or lack of motivation among others. Examples of ASB are:

» delinquent behaviour in public spaces;
» being rowdy and causing a nuisance in a neighbourhood;
» vandalism, graffiti and fly-posting;
» dealing and buying drugs on the street;
» dumping rubbish and abandoning cars;
» begging;
» anti-social drinking.

For safety reasons, parents must know where their children are going, when, with whom and for what purpose. Children should not be allowed to remain outside after an agreed time of day. This will prevent them from being involved in ASB themselves as well as protecting them from being victims of such crime.

Extremism and Radicalisation

The Muslim community is in the spotlight these days for radicalisation and extremism of our young people and many of our youth are accused of this. Many see this as an unhelpful over-generalisation. Allah describes the Muslim *ummah* in the Qur'an as *"ummatan wasatan"* – the community of the middle way (Surah al-Baqarah 2:143). In other words, it is a just and balanced religion that avoids extremes, either towards or away from religion. It is disturbing therefore that a section of our youth, however tiny, feels the need to wander from this middle path and take matters into their own hands.

It is praiseworthy that young people feel sympathy and anger at recent political events and injustices done to their co-religionists around the world. After all, when a part of the *ummah* is in pain, the rest of the *ummah* should share in that pain as if they were one body. But no matter how infuriated or angry one is, there is never any justification for being violent and maiming or taking the lives of innocent people regardless of their race or religion. Young people should know that it is never acceptable to step outside the principles of Islam or the bounds of the law, no matter what the provocation is.

Parents on their part need to keep a watchful but sensitive eye on whom their children are mixing with, what talks and circles they are attending, what material they are surfing on the net and what books they are reading. They should frankly exchange political and sensitive views with their children and understand what is causing the anger or any other feelings, but steer them in channelling those in ways that are positive for the community and society at large. Young people should be encouraged to read and listen more, but they should be guided on the authenticity of reading materials and trustworthiness of speakers.

Gangs

Gang violence among Muslim adolescents, especially boys, has become an increasing problem over the years in inner city areas. Sociologists and community leaders are of the opinion that social deprivation, massive unemployment, lack of motivation and under-achievement in education are linked to this problem. Some children are tempted to join gangs for a sense of belonging, or as a substitute for the sense of family they never had. Others do so because they feel they would lose their street credibility if they kept away. Many are influenced by drugs and the street culture.

Parents who give their children a warm and attentive family surrounding, spend quality time and work hard to ensure that their child's potential is achieved will be far less likely to face the problem of their child joining a gang.

Gang fighting: tackling the menace

If it were not because of some hard-working young Muslim activists, two gangs of Bangladeshi youth in two neighbourhoods of East London would have caused bloodshed among themselves some years ago. Nobody knew exactly what prompted these youth, having the same language and religious backgrounds, to come to that stage of taking revenge on each other with sophisticated weapons. The way they organised their groups was laudable, but it was a suicidal attempt and it was tarnishing the image of the community and creating internal disharmony.

Fortunately, before anyone was killed, some young Muslim activists successfully intervened. They belonged to the grass-roots and had influence over the leaders of both camps. That brought about three hundred of the young warriors to East London Mosque. Of course, a lot of background work was done beforehand and the choice of the mosque was also deliberate. When an emotional talk based on the teachings of Islam was delivered by a respected youth leader about the futility of their action and the responsibility of Muslim youth in building the community, very few could control their tears. They promised, one by one, that they would never again start a war against their own people. I still vividly remember the faces of the youths from both camps when they hugged each other after the speech.

Alcohol, Drugs and Smoking

Alcohol, drugs and smoking have the power to create addiction. Many adolescents drink and smoke in imitation of others or in defiance of their elders. Others are simply curious or want to 'be cool'. However, once a young person is addicted, and this does not take long, it is the start of a slippery slope to a number of other vices.

Drinking alcohol and taking drugs can lead to liver, heart and stomach problems, and smoking can lead to serious lung complaints. Apart from these devastating health effects, there are the social consequences and financial cost to the nation. Being under the influence of intoxicants may give rise to an array of behaviours such as sexual promiscuity, stealing to support an addiction, driving under the influence of intoxicants resulting in injury, death or a jail sentence.

Peer pressure can be very strong for some children, so parents need to be aware of whom their child is hanging around with. We need to talk to our children about drugs and related issues in a loving environment and remind them of Islamic viewpoints on intoxicants and the danger that they bring to people in terms of health, economy and morality. Young people should be warned that their safety and well-being are at stake with substance abuse.

Racism, Xenophobia and Islamophobia[5]

Racism and xenophobia are inhuman and abhorrent social diseases that have brought catastrophic human losses in history. Their products are slavery, colonialism, ruthless wars and killings. Nations were wiped out in the past because of their perceived racial inferiority. The two catastrophic World Wars in the last century were also rooted in the arrogance of racial superiority. Recently, the ethnic cleansing in the Balkans and some other parts of the world has so horrified the world and has its roots in blatant racism. In day-to-day life, in schools and workplaces, racism creates fear and distrust. It kills decent human behaviour and makes society loathsome.

Muslim children may experience prejudice because of their colour and religion and negative attitudes towards their beards and *hijabs*. At best, this is simply unpleasant and at worst it may affect their academic achievement and social performance. Muslim children who understand the beauty of the *deen*, the reasoning behind the *hijab* or beard and have the support of their family are much more likely to be comfortable within themselves and less likely to be affected by any negative comments directed against them.

The role of Muslim parents in the battle against racism and Islamophobia is two-fold. Firstly, we should equip our children with

---

5 Islamophobia refers to 'unfounded hostility towards Islam. It also refers to the practical consequences of such hostility in unfair discrimination against Muslim individuals and communities, and to the exclusion of Muslims from mainstream political and social affairs.' The Runnymede Trust, *Islamophobia: A Challenge for us all*, (London 1997), p4. Since 1997 the term has been frequently used by Muslims and others to describe anti-Muslim hate. Criticism of Islam and the Muslim community does not fall in this category. In the absence of any law prohibiting incitement to religious hatred, the phrase sometimes used by police is 'Islamophobic race hate crime'.

the knowledge and etiquette to defend themselves with dignity, to find racism and anti-religious sentiment abhorrent in all its forms and to fight against these diseases, wherever they may be. We need to educate them with the Qur'anic teaching on human beings' diversity which is for a divine purpose (Surah al-Hujurat 49:13). Young Muslims should be the carriers of the message that *taqwa*, not race, is the criterion of superiority in the eyes of Allah. They should be reminded that the battle against racism cannot be won with counter-racism or hatred, as some may be tempted to advocate. No matter how much Muslims suffer from racist and Islamophobic bigots, we should act with dignity, not revenge.

Sexual Mayhem

The three-letter word, sex, is now a determining factor in the lifestyles of post-modern permissive societies. It is a base desire which is indulged in at will, with no thought of the consequences to the individual or to society. Adultery and fornication, according to Islam, are two of the gravest wrong actions that a person can commit. Allah, the Almighty, has not only prohibited adultery, but commanded people not to go near it (Surah al-Isra 17:32). Sexual libido is inherent in human nature and man has been given a higher share of sexual aggressiveness for a reason. However, it should not be allowed to go wild, but to be tamed and used appropriately and responsibly.

Contrary to what people with laissez-faire attitudes say, sexual promiscuity is not just a matter of personal enjoyment, but has wide-reaching social implications. Sexually transmitted diseases such as HIV, Gonorrhoea, Chlamydia and Syphilis are on the increase causing individual discomfort at best and infertility and terminal illness at worst. The sexual assault and rape of women is commonplace as are underage sex and teenage pregnancies. The solution is being sought in superficial measures, such as free distribution of 'morning after pills' for girls and condoms for boys. There is a rigid unwillingness to address the root of the problem. As a result, boys and girls are becoming parents without acquiring a sense of responsibility and accountability. Their relationship is only skin deep, and there is little idea of planning for a long-term relationship or family bonding. Marriage is losing its sanctity as the source of permanent relationship between man and woman, and divorce is increasing at an alarming rate, while living together without marriage is becoming the norm.

Permissive sexual practices are now so commonplace that it is hard to shield children from the messages that they receive on a daily basis. The best that parents can do is to arm them with Islamic knowledge and a sense of responsibility. Parents must be open but sensitive in their discussion about sex and sexuality with their children, explaining its place in a Muslim's life and the benefits of not giving into base desires for instant pleasure. Young people should know that not only are adultery and fornication *haram* in themselves but all that leads to them is *haram* as well. This includes looking at books, magazines, websites and films of an explicit sexual nature, gatherings where men and women are dressed in a revealing manner to impress the opposite sex and even gazing lustfully at someone of the opposite sex.

Homosexuality

On top of this, the issue of homosexuality, or same-sex relationships, is gaining momentum all over the world. In recent decades gay rights lobbies have been wielding much influence in the social and political arena of many developed societies. As a result, homosexuality is gradually becoming an accepted social norm in many countries with same-sex marriage or civil partnerships now being legally accepted in many countries. Giving these the same legal status as marriage may be the social trend in some societies, but it is not acceptable in any transcendental religion. As in the two other Abrahamic faiths, Islam is unequivocal in maintaining that a sexual relationship can only be between a man and a woman in marriage.

Before this issue divides our community as it has done others before, Muslims should be united in arguing the case against homosexuality, albeit in a civilised manner. Islam does not promote violence or incite hatred against any people because of their lifestyle, but Muslims have a duty to argue for what they believe, with patience and wisdom (Surah Fussilat 41:34). Muslim parents should educate themselves on this and be clear in their own understanding before they educate their children. The issue has been mentioned in a number of places in the Qur'an, for example, Surah al-A'raf 7:80-84, Surah Hud 11:77-83, Surah al-Naml 27:54-56, Surah Ankabut 29:28-34 and Surah al-Saffat 37:133-137.

Paedophilia

Young people are like plants that need nurturing, not misuse or abuse. Unfortunately, every community has its share of criminals who abuse vulnerable children when they deserve nothing but innocent love and affection.

Paedophilia is not only inhuman, but a heinous crime that destroys the innocence of children at a tender age. Some paedophiles are even bent on taking the precious lives of young children once they have molested them. In civilised societies the agencies of law and order rely on the civic responsibility of people. It is a trust among members of the society. Paedophiles are criminals who take advantage of this social trust. It is imperative that parents know whose care and trust their child is held in. Children should be told what unacceptable behaviour is on the part of an adult, whether related or otherwise. Parents should be open and responsive so that children can come and discuss any concerns, should they arise.

Domestic Violence

Young people seem to be getting more and more angry and frustrated nowadays. Whether because of employment issues, substance abuse or family pressures, an increasing number of young Muslim men are taking out their frustrations verbally and physically on the people around them. Domestic violence in sections of the Muslim community is increasing. While victims are still generally women, the number of male victims is on the increase. Parents need to tell their adolescent boys and girls of the good nature of the righteous predecessors of Islam in their family and social life. It is an Islamic teaching to see life partners and children as a trust and privilege that are not to be mishandled and misused. Parents should encourage their children to release their emotion, anger or frustration in a healthy and positive way, such as sports and should themselves live such a life that their children never witness violence within their own home. Treating each other kindly and respectfully is the essence of Islamic character.

Materialism and the Loss of Values

Over the centuries, materialism has pushed aside Christianity from its position of moral influence in the West and society has given into amorality. The post-modern West has seen the rise of moral relativism in which there is little room for clear values in life. The result is a moral maze where universal values, such as honesty, fidelity, morality and a sense of justice have been pushed aside in favour of individualism, egocentrism and the desire to enjoy oneself whatever the consequences. Children pick up materialistic and hedonistic attitudes from a young age; ask young people about their ambition in life and many will respond that they want to be rich or to simply enjoy themselves.

TV, computers and other gadgets are keeping people away from personal and social relationships to the point where young people do not know how to interact any more. Fewer families are eating together or spending quality time with each other.

Increasing importance is attached to material belongings, large houses, fast cars and fashionable clothes. Men and women are fighting each other to achieve this lifestyle. Allah has given man and woman dignity in their own characteristic features and their role is complementary in this world. While a woman has not been stopped from working and earning her own money in Islam, her role as a mother should never be undermined. Paradise lies under the feet of mothers. Society puts a heavy burden on girls if they are made to compete with men in their careers, made to look attractive and at the same time to take care of the household and be mothers.

Muslim boys and girls are getting married later these days, some obviously for genuine reasons. At the same time, some couples are finding it harder to stay together, even when they have married out of choice. This can be attributed to young people's individualistic lifestyle, general impatience and their inability to compromise on family affairs and sacrifice personal opinions.

Another victim of the materialist secular lifestyle has been Islamic etiquette. The lack of *adab* in relationships is apparent among many young Muslims in the West, even among youth engaged in Islamic activities. Caring and responsible behaviour is the essence of social life. Muslims throughout history have emulated the model character of the Prophet Muhammad ﷺ and created societies full of love, compassion and concern for others, but it seems that egotism and self-centred individualism are penetrating into the behaviour of Muslims, even many supposed Islamic activists. Young Muslims are failing to maintain the right balance between the rights of Allah and the rights of human beings.

What can parents do? Firstly, we must pull ourselves out of the trap of materialism so that we can motivate our youngsters. Simply eating and praying together, spending quality time as a family will teach children that contentment does not come from material possessions but from within. Increased positive and respectful social interaction between parents and children will provide young people an example of how best to behave in a way that embodies service to others, kindness and respect.

Parents must explain the role of men and women to their boys and girls, so they can fulfil these to the best of their abilities as the parents of tomorrow. Both girls and boys should be educated, in the *deen* and in worldly knowledge, to the best of their ability. Muslims need to work with others to elevate motherhood as the greatest profession so that children can enjoy the company of their mothers when needed, with undivided love and attention. Young sons need to be taught that the beauty of a woman lies in her modesty, chastity and her understanding of Islam, not in her skin colour, hairstyle or waist size. Similarly, daughters must know that the looks and income of a man are not his defining characteristics, but his practice of the *deen* is.

Marriage should be viewed as a comforting and dynamic partnership to be enjoyed but one that requires hard work, respect, compromise and sacrifice. It is a lifelong commitment for the preservation of one's chastity, the fulfilment of half of one's *deen* and the procreation of children in a loving, stable environment as part of a team. When we instil these attitudes in our children from an early age and portray them through our own actions, only then can we hope that our children will be successful within their own lives.

Agony of a Muslim Mother

"My sons and daughters are alhamdulillah involved in Islamic activities and I have been active in Islamic work for over three decades. I am happy about that, but unfortunately they are so busy that I do not see them much. It seems that they have little interest in household chores. In fact, sometimes they behave as if they are guests in their own house. We have to do most of their chores – cooking, washing, cleaning, etc. We did this when they were young and we were stronger, but we are getting older now. We have talked to the children on some occasions. They do not deny their responsibility and keep on promising they will do household chores, but there is little accord in their words and actions. It is so sad. What is happening to young people today?"

Fighting the Ills

Allah, in His wisdom, has instilled in man the dual nature of evil and piety (Surah al-Shams 91:8). In a healthy society, piety is encouraged and promoted to flourish and evil suppressed. Piety needs nourishment and a conducive environment, not only for its growth but also for its survival. Throughout human history schools and institutions have been established to create good human beings. No school was ever established to train rapists, paedophiles, gang fighters, drug users or killers. But when society loses its anchor and direction, they grow and multiply.

To begin with, a few people begin to promote their small vices. When left unopposed, society gradually begins to accommodate them and accept them as the norm. The boundaries keep being pushed until society slides into degeneration. The most vulnerable victims of this downfall are young people.

The challenge of fighting social ills is enormous and this is not just a Muslim problem; it is common to the whole of society. As such, the Muslim attempt to challenge and minimise these ills should be two-pronged. Muslims should join any initiative that seeks to minimise or eradicate violence and obscenity in the media and the entertainment industry as well as other social ills in the society where they live. For an effective challenge, we need to widen our partnership to fight for spiritual regeneration in our communities. This is only possible if we are fully aware of what is going on around us and proactively interact and engage with other faith and non-faith communities. Mere moaning about the affairs of society is not helpful. The sooner we understand this and act, the better.

However, on a family level, parents should try to create a protective shield around their own children through various means and expend energy into their parenting efforts in order to prevent the causes that can lead to children becoming sucked into the moral black hole. Some useful tips are:

» **Adhere** to the principles and tenets of **Islam**. This will provide the boundaries within which parents can raise their children.

» **Listen** to children when they talk and give them undivided attention. Do not interrupt them. Do not dismiss their concerns, however trivial they may seem, but treat them with importance.

» Be prepared to **compromise**. It is not reasonable to expect children to obey every command of their parents. Parents and children need to compromise and negotiate with each other in order to find a solution or result where both sides are satisfied.

» Be **consistent** in the parenting approach. Differing behaviour from a parent or difference of opinion between one parent and another will only serve to confuse teenagers.

» Be **honest** in speech and **transparent** in actions. Efforts to hide from children, especially adolescents, can result in them losing confidence in their parents.

» **Apologise** for any mistakes you may have committed. Children should know that their parents are not perfect. When parents apologise for a mistake, this gives children confidence in their sense of justice and they cannot view them as unfair.

» **Ignore** their small **mistakes** and allow children to have their **own space** to rid themselves of their embarrassment, anger or frustration.

» **Share** decision-making in the family. Teenagers often come up with clever ideas that can help. At the same time, inclusion in decision-making helps them feel part of the decision and more willing to co-operate.

» Do not be bossy with children, rather take the time to **talk** with them and **explain** things to them.

» **Recognise** children's worth and **reward** them for any good that they do. This gives them inner happiness and encourages them to keep on doing good things. It also gives them the assurance that they are valued. However, praise should be given for positive effort or action and parents must be careful not to bribe and spoil them.

» Build a sound and lasting relationship with children, on the basis of **love** and **respect**.

» Make *du'a* for them. Guidance is from Allah alone and Muslims always rely on Allah for their actions and outcomes. Continuous *du'a* (supplication) for the guidance of children is essential for believing parents.

Chapter Three

Motivating to Excel

Make things easy and do not make them difficult. Make them calm and do not make them feel aversion.
(Sahih al-Bukhari)

Human Beings are Unique

Human beings have been granted free will and the criterion to judge between right and wrong. Yet it is these things that got Adam and Hawwa, peace be upon them, into trouble before they arrived on earth. The only thing that saved them from the ultimate downfall was sincere repentance; a lesson that we should all take from this story.

We are fortunate that Allah has created the world full of challenges for us. Without challenges, our minds would stagnate and become despondent at the monotony and we would descend into a state of lethargic self-centredness. Challenges motivate people to think and lead the way forward for change and, as a result, society becomes dynamic and adventurous. Of course, there will be mistakes but it is through these mistakes that progress is made. So, what is motivation and what does it do? Broadly speaking, motivation is:

» the ability to drive and inspire;
» strong will or stamina, a real determination to see things through;
» the passion to make a difference;
» a vision of success;
» the capacity to implement the vision in a manner that is manageable;
» commitment to continuous monitoring and evaluation.

Motivation is at the heart of human success. It is the inner urge, enthusiasm, passion and fire that sustain commitment to follow things through. Motivation is central to commitment, but by nature, it is intangible and cannot be measured. The fire of motivation needs fuel, which parents, elders and teachers need to provide at the beginning of children's lives. So what makes young people tick? What motivates them to do something? Is human behaviour driven by physical needs, social, egotistic or self-actualisation needs, as Maslow and his co-thinkers proposed? Are human beings inherently positive or negative about doing something? Are they intrinsically good or bad in life?

It may seem that these questions are merely philosophical, but they do hold great importance in our personal and social lives. From the dawn of civilisation, people have pondered the answers to these questions, but outside of Divine revelation the answers are not complete.

Following the advent of Islam, the Arabs and other nations in their heydays, displayed monumental human qualities that helped shape the world in the way it is today. The reason was because they were highly motivated. Why? Because the depth of their *iman* was vast and they had found a higher purpose for their life on earth. Later on, as they lost the spirit of Islam they lost their direction. They became stagnant in their thinking and passive in their actions. All the qualities that made them great - their competence, pride, self-determination, sense of responsibility, creativity, innovation, initiative and confidence - gradually evaporated.

Allah has given each human being tremendous potential. Each one of us is unique, with individual characteristics and infinite variables that affect our lives. The environment that we are exposed to either causes our potential to flower and blossom or to remain dormant and unfulfilled. Thus the environment that parents nurture their children in has a direct effect on how they are and what they can become.

How can young people be motivated to achieve their potential and be the very best they can be? How can Muslim adolescents be made more creative, positive and motivated in their thinking and action so that they can regenerate their community and serve humanity? The answer is through encouragement, positive role models, a balanced attitude towards their growth and a vision of success. There will be failures along the way but the conscientious parent knows how to manage these in such a way that the core of the person, his or her self-esteem, is not damaged.

Self-Esteem

Self-esteem is a positive life-view that reflects one's self-image, self-awareness and self-confidence. In believers, self-esteem is indicative of esteem for Allah, since being Allah's creations we must have the highest opinion of ourselves. How can parents measure their child's self-esteem? The following personal qualities are useful indicators and parents can grade their child for each quality, if they wish.[6]

adaptable	adventurous	ambitious
cheerful	conscientious	considerate
dependable	determined	friendly
helpful	honest	loyal
lively	neat	patient
polite	popular	punctual
responsible	thoughtful	trustworthy
virtuous	confident	energetic
enthusiastic		

Every child is special and needs to be treated as such. It is human nature that babies and adults alike need to be noticed, recognised and respected for who they are by their loved ones. The Messenger of Allah ﷺ understood this perfectly and, as such, gave every Companion his full attention to such an extent that every one of them considered themselves to be closest to the Prophet ﷺ. Parents need to build on the positive aspects of their children and praise them for their good behaviour and qualities in order to encourage them. But praise must be genuine, timely and deserved. Indiscriminate praise or flattery is detrimental in the long run, as it can make children complacent or spoilt.

Children are learners and making mistakes is all too natural. This is something that good parents will take in their stride. As they gradually enter into the world of responsibility, children learn from their own mistakes. Small inconsequential mistakes can be

---

6 From Disaffection to Social Inclusion: A Social Skills Preparation for Active Citizenship and Employment, John Huskins, p50, 2000, UK

overlooked, however intentional or major mistakes must not be allowed to go unnoticed. Correcting a child within a supportive and understanding atmosphere while they are young is better for the young person than learning the hard way from others when they are older. In correcting their child, parents should deal with the situation at hand and in context without bringing up past mistakes. Kindness and respect will always achieve the desired result more effectively than harshness and humiliation. In any case, parents must not put their child down or make demeaning comments to them as this can lead to their failure in future life.

Parental expectation is also an important factor in motivating children and creating self-confidence in them. Too low an expectation can shatter the self-image and pride of children, while too high an expectation can over-pressure them and ruin their chances of success. The level of expectation should match the abilities of the child as well as their temperament.

Parents with high-achieving children should closely watch their physical, emotional and mental development. Fast-track children offer fast-track challenges and they need creative interventions so that they can engage themselves without being bored. On the other hand, parents with under-achieving children need to make sure they get proper care and the necessary educational support. Phenomenal work has already been done in developed countries in the field of Special Educational Needs (SEN). In recent years inclusive education and social inclusion have become widely discussed issues. Inclusive education creates an inclusive society, in which everybody contributes and nobody becomes a burden on others. If children display learning, behavioural or other difficulties, physical or mental handicaps, or special talents they should not be stigmatised. What they need is professional support and special care. Many children with special needs have turned out to be highly gifted children who later contributed to civilisation.

Encouragement

Children are generally impressionable, idealistic and impulsive, as they have yet to come to terms with the realities and complexities of life. They need continuous encouragement, appreciation and recognition from elders. If this is missing, they can get lost in their motivational journey. Labelling them with terms such as, 'useless', 'failure', 'hopeless', 'idiot' and 'dumb' can paralyse their motivation. It is very easy to compare one's children with others' or even with their own siblings, but insensitive comparison can undermine their confidence and create an inferiority complex.

Performance in school or exam results can be a cause of friction, especially with parents of Asian origin. It is unreasonable to expect a child to achieve top results in every exam and every piece of schoolwork throughout their academic life. Too much pressure in the early school years can result in children 'burning out' when they come to national exam level. However, gifted and talented children can lose motivation if they are inadequately challenged or teased for being clever or holding unconventional ideas.

Children who lose their motivation may not just suffer from low self-confidence. On a deeper level, they may start to develop self-destructive behaviour such as self-harm or start acting up because they feel rejected. Parents may misinterpret this and make insensitive remarks or lessen their affection and understanding towards their children. This will only make things worse. Dejected children need careful handling. Parents need to be especially careful and sensitive about how they speak and interact with their children so that they begin to feel more positive about themselves and are able to rediscover their self-worth. We need to remind our children that all human beings have tremendous potential and encourage them as they try to achieve it.

Positive Role Modelling

Positive role modelling provides invisible psychological leadership to young people. Islamic history is full of people, including male and female youth, who were role models in the past. Prophet Muhammad ﷺ is the finest role model for people of all ages:

> *You have an excellent model in the Messenger of Allah,*
> *for all who put their hope in Allah and the Last Day and*
> *remember Allah much.* (Surah al-Ahzab 33:21)

Who are the role models of today? Muslim adolescents in the West, and for that matter anywhere in the world now, open their eyes and step into a world full of disappointment. The environment around them is ripe with the failure and impotence of the *ummah* and its marginalisation in the world arena. There is little confidence in the present Muslim leadership and the number of role models is frustratingly minimal. This vacuum has been filled with celebrity role models that have a singular philosophy of life, 'eat, drink, and be merry'. They are the products of a consumer culture and a materialistic view of life.

The absence of positive role models around young people, in the community and in broader society, has been a destabilising factor among Muslim youth. Achieving success is important for children, but they have to know what they can achieve and understand what success means. They need the confidence to plan and the competence to achieve. Above all, they need to have someone set them a benchmark for success that they can emulate or even surpass. Who is better and closer to them than their own parents?

Even with the presence of a role model, children cannot automatically make the connection from where they are to where they would like to be. They need help in setting their own targets with people that they trust. Parents should help set targets that are high, but not so much as to be off-putting, and set goals that can be achieved within manageable timeframes. After all, the longest of journeys consists of many small steps.

We also need to instil in our children a sense of the real meaning of success. Allah has set in human hearts a perpetual quest for pleasure and tranquillity that can only be achieved through meaningful work. The Prophet of Islam ﷺ, with his captivating character, and as 'a witness and a conveyer of good tidings and a warner' (Surah al-Ahzab 33:45), presented a sky-high vision to his Companions, the first generation of Muslims. They, in turn, became role models for the rest of humanity. In addition, both the substance and style of Islam's message created self-motivation in the thirsty hearts of Arabia. Thus, deep understanding of Islam motivates a Muslim to move forward.

The glad tidings of Paradise and the warning of the Hellfire in the Hereafter are the motivating factors for believing people. They are guided to struggle for good and the welfare of others, solely for the pleasure of Allah and not for their own self-fulfilment. There must be a vision and hope, without which human beings are doomed to passivity and lethargy. The Qur'an has mentioned the multiplicity of rewards (Surah al-Fath 48:29), which catapult Muslims towards making even greater efforts. The ultimate motivation derives from the fact that Allah, the Creator, will reveal Himself to His obedient slaves in Paradise. That is the pinnacle of success for a human being.

A Balanced Growth

Success in parenting comes when parents address the needs of the whole child: mental, physical, emotional as well as spiritual. Most importantly, parents need to impart to their children a love of Allah and His Messenger ﷺ and pride in Islam. Children should be imparted with worldly knowledge and encouraged to think and reflect, rather than indulge in the rote learning that has crippled creativity in most Muslim countries.

Maintaining a healthy balance in one's life is not always easy and it is easier said than done. As adolescent children often tend to follow their role models, parents need to link them with such people, preferably living among them, who have positive and balanced views of life and at the same time are themselves positive and balanced. This should be supplemented with a meaningful study of the *Seerah* (life of the Prophet Muhammad ﷺ) so that young Muslims can draw inspiration from him and come to love him and emulate his blessed life. There are numerous great figures in Islamic history that provide good role models and motivation for young people.

Nothing Succeeds Like Success

Every parent dreams of success for their child, no matter what their view of success. Children who feel successful develop a positive self-image. Success, according to Islam, is 'the good of the world and the Hereafter' (Surah al-Baqarah 2:201), both in balance and not one at the expense of the other. The Prophets of Allah were the teachers of humanity. Prophet Shu'aib ﷺ is quoted in the Qur'an as saying, 'My success is with Allah alone' (Surah Hud 11:88). This is the key for a Muslim: in knowing that success is only by and from Allah. Conscientious parents strive to do the best for their children on their part by providing a stable and trusting environment and giving them a good education.

Parents should certainly look for good schools and educational institutions for their children, but home is the best school and real education starts at home when children are in their formative years. These are the years between birth and the age of seven, according to Khalifah Umar ﷺ. This is the stage when parents need to invest most of their time and energy in giving company to their children and in educating them through play.

Step-by-Step Development[7]

Human qualities such as willpower, perseverance, fortitude and self-discipline are the ingredients of success in life. They do not come suddenly or by chance, they need nurturing and step-by-step development. Not all human beings possess these qualities to the same degree and indeed some can lack one or several of these qualities from childhood. However, a positive environment at home and surroundings can compensate for such inadequacies to some extent and parents have a major role to play in inculcating these qualities in their children.

Children need encouragement to explore, be adventurous and also to feel relaxed. They need recognition, reassurance and quality time with their parents. If parents can genuinely instil in their children love and trust for Allah and His Messenger ﷺ, a self-belief, self-efficacy and self-direction in their character, that will lead them towards a confident life. Parents cannot be with their children forever, but they can sow the seeds of success in their lives by:

» showing an interest, but not becoming intrusive;
» offering direction, but not being dictatorial;
» encouraging talents, yet keeping them in control;
» containing, but not confining them;
» establishing routines, but by building flexibility;
» supporting and encouraging, but not controlling and pushing;
» offering choice, but avoiding manipulation.

Parents should not demand too much from their children too quickly, but they need to be stretched in their efforts so they can make steady progress. The world can be a tough and competitive place and the path through life can be thorny. This makes life challenging and adventurous, but enjoyable. Life is tough and one must have a

---

7 Motivating Your Child: Tools and Tactics to Help Your Child be a Self-starter, Elizabeth Hartley-Brewer, pp2-5, 1998, London

determination to succeed, in the sense of success which has been outlined above. The legendary Andalusian Imam Qurtubi once said, 'A first class will and a second class brain wins over a first class brain and a second class will.'

Managing Failure

Human beings often experience failure. Some temporary success can also lead to failure. Failure should not be taken as the end of an endeavour, rather as an opportunity to reflect, learn from it and to understand ourselves. In some cases, failure can be a pillar of success. The Islamic principle is that we strive to our utmost and then we rely on Allah for the outcome. For a Muslim who tries hard there is no failure, even if that apparently seems to be the case. Whatever we do in our lives with the intention of pleasing our Lord, we are rewarded on the basis of our intentions and our efforts. However, human beings always look for immediate gain (Surah al-Saff 61:13), for we are ever hasty (Surah al-Isra 17:11).

Throughout their lives, it is inevitable that children may fail at something. Parents should be able to separate the failure from the child. One cannot be good at everything, so failure in one area does not necessarily mean failure in life. For children with positive outlooks on life, failure can sharpen their determination to win over a problem and this increases their motivation. Through failure they learn new skills and techniques. It increases their self-awareness. Parents need to be supportive through such times, allowing children to learn from their setbacks and come through stronger and wiser than before.

Children are energetic human beings, not puppets or dolls. They are creative and talented and have hopes and aspirations, fears and anxieties. Parents are there to nurture the whole child. If they want their children to be self-starters they have to guide them consistently, supplicate for them and refrain from being negative.

Enthusing the Young Mind

Parents are not necessarily required to have a high degree of formal education nor do they need to be wealthy to help their children flourish. These assets may offer some added advantage, but are not essential for motivating young people. What we do need is understanding, passion and quality time to make sure that the home, school and community environments push young people towards being self-motivated.

Ordinary parents can enthuse their children in extraordinary ways if only they show enough enthusiasm to inspire their young ones and spend time with them. The language of love is understood by all, and parental love for their children and an interest in their children's well-being is infectious.

At School

Children need a good school where they feel at ease and receive continuous encouragement through its:

» learning culture;
» positive ethos;
» high expectation;
» set of goals in curriculum areas;
» recognition of rights and responsibilities;
» clear, consistent and fair discipline;
» relationship based on respect and trust;
» positive competition;
» involvement in creative activities.

Strong discipline, sound behaviour policy, creative extra-curricular activities and good academic results on the one hand and a safe environment on the other keep children more content in the school environment.

At Home

Parents should make sure that their young ones feel loved and wanted at all times. They should experience that the ownership of success is entirely Allah's, but at the same time, be constructively reminded or sensitively criticised for any mistakes. Childhood is a time of exploration, discovery and experimentation and it is the nature of humans to err. In Islam, there is single reward for effort and double reward for success. If they know the framework of discipline and the Islamic boundaries of behaviour, children will find it easy to keep within their limits and achieve within it. As parents, we should:

» not put a barrier between our children and us;
» have a sense of humour so that children get along with us. People without humour are dull;
» trust our children to do things;
» encourage children to take responsibility for a task;
» observe their level of maturity before asking them to do a job;
» teach through example, not by words only;
» make choices visible and available to them;
» break the goal into bite-size, achievable targets. Small wins provide a sense of achievement, give self-confidence and have a multiplier effect;
» introduce them to new ideas. We should see the merit in their ideas, even if they contradict ours;
» accept their mistakes. They should start from what they are and not what we want them to be;
» be available to talk to them, even when under pressure;
» praise and recognise children.

While praising, we should be:

» specific about we are praising them for;
» straightforward and honest. We should not use conditional words, like 'if' and 'but';
» spontaneous;
» overt in physical expression, such as smiles, hugs and kisses;
» generous in giving them credit, even if they got help from us;
» measured. We should not spoil them with too much praise.

In the Community

Where individuals and families struggle with their children the community should try to compensate. In Muslim societies, imams, mosque leaders and local civic leaders can play an enormous role in guiding the community towards maintaining Islamic values and also for the overall prosperity of the community. These people become even more important in a pluralist and secular environment where religion and culture are under continuous scrutiny.

The Muslim community, through mosques, Islamic centres and other organisations should:

» invest their energy in educating and training the youth to become good Muslims and conscientious citizens;
» open up so that young people feel encouraged to participate;
» take proactive steps to connect with young people and involve them in running these organisations;
» try to bring more professionalism in running projects and events by involving young people;
» make sure young people feel ownership in the community so that they grow as confident Muslims;
» encourage young people to discharge their Islamic and civic responsibility in a pluralist society.

Chapter Four

Home Environment

The Messenger of Allah ﷺ kissed Hasan ibn Ali while al-Aqra ibn Habis at-Tamimi was sitting with him. Al-Aqra observed, 'I have ten children and I have not kissed any of them.' The Messenger of Allah ﷺ looked at him and said, 'Whoever does not show mercy will not be shown mercy.'
(Al-Adab al-Mufrad al-Bukhari)

The Importance of the Home Environment

Secondary school age children spend a relatively longer period of their lives in school and outside the home, compared to primary school children. In addition, they have a greater degree of freedom and are exposed to more of the world around them, good and bad. The school ethos, teachers and peers, TV programmes, the internet, and the outside world are constantly shaping their thoughts and influencing their actions. The other great influences in the lives of adolescents are their home environment, parents, extended family and social interaction.

In a society where schools no longer teach moral and religious values, where academic institutions are seen to be places in which to gain a worldly education only, and success lies in status and wealth and job titles, then the importance of the home environment becomes paramount in shaping the spiritual side of children. A person is greater than the grades they achieve or the job that they do. The measure of a person lies in their *taqwa* and their nobility of character.

Both mothers and fathers have their vital role to play in achieving this by actively engaging with their sons and daughters during this challenging journey of life. To begin with, parents' own behaviour and actions should be exemplary so that children immediately have access to role models within their own home, rather than being tempted by celebrities. Secondly, parents need to address the specific needs and issues of their child. These issues will be different to those experienced by parents themselves in their childhood and will vary from child to child. There is no 'one size fits all' solution. Parents, therefore, need to be creative and forward thinking so that they can guide their children through the misleading maze of confusing messages around them.

Home is the base for a child; the place where they are loved unconditionally, where they are understood and reassured. The home environment 'charges' the child with confidence so that they can go out into the world and play a positive role. This can only come about when parents are strong in human and Islamic qualities, yet flexible and loving in their approach. At a time when children are receiving mixed messages all around them, the lifestyle at home should be singular in its aims. Parents who like to teach Islam but do not practice it or put cultural considerations above religious ones, will only confuse their young ones. That is not to say that culture is a negative feature; it is a part of one's identity and influences some aspects of life. However, it should not be blindly followed where it goes against religious teachings.

Adolescence is not an isolated phase in a child's life. The time preceding it and its challenges have an effect on adolescent life and so parenting should not begin in earnest at adolescence but as early as possible. One of the most important aspects in Islam is religious practices and, although they become obligatory only in post-puberty life, they should be introduced to children at a younger age. In a society where following religious practices can be seen as embarrassing and backward, children need to understand what they practise and feel proud of their religion. This means that parents need to equip their children with knowledge of the basic practices, an understanding of how these fit into the religion and the spirit behind them. Children should start performing their *salah* by the age of seven, practice *sawm* (fasting) and start wearing *hijab* before they enter into puberty so that by the time they enter into puberty these acts become second nature. The key to fostering love for the religion is kindness, patience and compassion in matters of the *deen*. Harshness turns away hearts and sudden imposition of Islamic practices at puberty may have negative effects. Necessary groundwork is thus vital.

However, everything in Islam must be viewed in context and in order of priority. Muslims never compromise on the core beliefs and practices of Islam. Good social behaviour or Islamic manners (*adab*), cleanliness (*taharah*) and modesty (*haya*), along with honesty, integrity and hard work are fundamentally important for a Muslim. Without these basic human qualities a Muslim can never attain pleasure from Allah and bring social well-being. There is room for flexibility and accommodation in the non-essential elements of religion. Placing disproportionate importance on external expression, for example, dress, at the expense of the core values of Islam is against the spirit of religion. At the end of the day, whether a Muslim has become a good human being and an emissary of Allah is important. Just as the quality of fruit indicates the worth of a tree, adolescent behaviour reflects family background.

Despite the different environments at home and at school, they should not be seen as diametrically opposing each other. Both have positive roles to play in shaping each unique individual and have a complementary relationship for the well-being of the adolescent. Home liaison has become one of the most important and positive initiatives to improving secondary school performance and children's behaviour. Through Parent Teacher Associations, parents' evenings and other mechanisms, secondary schools try to build strong links with parents and the local community. Needless to say that this is very much compatible with the Islamic way of dealing with children, as it is holistic and vital for children's stability and self-respect in their adolescence.

Quality Time with Children

Creating a wholesome home environment requires constant hard work and attention from both the father and the mother. The demands of adolescence in a permissive society put a lot of pressure on children as well as parents. Parents need to spend regular, quality time with their children for which there is absolutely no substitute. This is essential for building a sound and deeper bond between each child and each parent. However, a mother's role in creating a home, showering it with tenderness, love and understanding and keeping the family strongly anchored to Islam is undeniable.

Sadly in the struggle for survival and earning a decent living, quality time becomes a scarcity for many parents. Over-stretched and overlapping work schedules hinder parents' interactions with their children. In traditional families, the mother stayed at home to manage the household and be a constant reassuring presence for her children. Nowadays many mothers either choose to or are pressured to work to maintain the family lifestyle or to supplement income. In single parent families, the situation is even more difficult. As a result, children spend their time with TV, computers and other hi-tech gadgets. This creates a distance or barrier between children and their parents and makes effective communication even harder, especially when parents are unaware of what their child is exposed to. It is essential both parents recognise that, although their adolescent is no longer physically dependant, they need just as much attention for their spiritual and emotional well-being. Both parents should work towards a strategy which puts their child at the centre of family and allows them to spend that all-important quality time together. This may include getting outside help for the household chores, reducing work hours or working flexible hours, and enlisting the help of other members of the family such as grandparents, if available.

Experience has shown that children with both responsible parents around them generally grow up with happiness and confidence. Children, particularly boys, whose fathers play an effective role develop greater self-esteem. They are more likely to do better in their education and less likely to be involved in anti-social behaviour. Muslim fathers need to come to the forefront of the parenting effort together with mothers. In the midst of negative portrayals and numerous challenges Muslim boys are facing now it is absolutely important that fathers do play their part in building their community.

Adolescent boys and girls have specific emotional demands for all sorts of things in their life in transition. Some of them are embarrassing and children do not share these with anyone except those close to them. Some adolescents cannot cope with all these emotional demands, and as a result boys generally act out and girls act in. During the adolescent period a confident and loving mother can provide emotional support to her daughter, especially on feminine issues. In the same way, a confident and caring father can also be of immense help to his son, especially on masculine affairs. Without a close relationship this is impossible, as children will feel inhibited about opening up to their parents.

Creating a Muslim Youth Culture

The world is now very small and interdependent. Societies in the East and the West are gradually becoming more pluralistic. Muslims, in the past, co-existed with other communities amicably and in many Western countries they are now living peacefully with others in local communities. Young Muslims need exposure to the wider society. That is the spirit of Islam. They need friends from all sections of the community, but they should be guided in finding close friends whose values of life are similar to their own or at least not antagonistic.

Taking children to mosques and Islamic centres from a young age, when children are able to maintain *adab* of the mosque, opens the door to a wider world with people of different races and languages. Mosques have always been the hub of social and educational activities in Islamic history. Unfortunately, many mosques today are quiet and are even locked outside prayer times. Regeneration of the *ummah* will remain a dream if mosques are used for ritual prayers alone. The mosque of the Messenger of Allah ﷺ in Madinah was the hub of society and so our mosques must be today.

In addition to congregational prayers and Qur'an classes, mosques should organise a host of activities, for example, sports, discussion groups and supplementary classes for both men and women. Mosques and community organisations must move away from their traditional reluctance to involve young Muslims and include them in community affairs. Imams, preferably 'home-grown', should be competent in communication skills and should have basic knowledge and understanding of their community and wider society in order to be able to relate to both young and old. Improving standards in mosques, running them professionally and engaging young people should be at the forefront of mosque agendas.

Mosques, weekend schools or community clubs can occasionally arrange for day trips and weekend or holiday camps, for fun and learning so that children can grow together as Muslims. They create opportunities to make friendships with others, which is very important for their social life. Children easily make and break friends and through this they learn about themselves and the world around them. A peer group of good Muslims friends will encourage each other to do common good and they are often more powerful than academic instructions. On the other hand, parents should be careful that their children avoid the company of other children who can mislead them or encourage them to do wrong things. Young people are generally prone to the fashionable 'youth culture' of the day, in reality a 'culture' created by market forces for their own profit. The Prophet Muhammad ﷺ has warned:

A person is upon the deen of his friend, so see whom you take as a friend. (Abu Dawud, At-Tirmidhi and Ahmad)

If time and finances permit, family holidays should be taken in places of historical and Islamic significance, *Umrah* is obviously the best choice. Bringing the stories of the past to life through these visits will create added motivation and inspiration in children.

The best way to harness the potential of Muslim children is to involve them in regular Islamic circles from an early age, where they can be engaged in a host of activities. The Prophet Muhammad ﷺ revived and initiated social welfare work through an association called *Hilf al-Fudul*, in his youth. Parents should encourage their children to join good groups related to mosques or reputable Muslim organisations. There are now many groups that cater for children in their teens, but children need to start their communal responsibilities earlier, even from junior school age. Junior groups can engage young children in challenging activities and create motivation in them to grow within a sound Islamic environment.

Muslim parents need to give their youth effective support so that these young people feel valued in their own communities, mosques and also in the wider society. This is an investment to get something back from them. For this to happen, parents must resist the temptation to over-protect their children.

Useful Tips

Creating a positive home environment is a mammoth task and it can be difficult to know where to begin. These are a few points that will help in this regard:

- Establish prayer on time. When possible, fathers should take their sons to join in congregational prayers. Otherwise, pray together at home.
- Recite the Qur'an every day. It will bring blessing to the home and peace to the reader and the listener.
- Refer to the Qur'an and *Sunnah* when needing advice about any issue. These two central sources contain all the information that human beings need in their everyday lives and should always be the reference points for Muslims.
- Follow Allah's guidance and the *Sunnah* of the Prophet ﷺ ourselves in our daily activities. This includes much remembrance of Allah, supplication and the *masnoon du'a* (supplications from the *Sunnah*) for any event or incident, as taught by the Prophet ﷺ.
- Exemplify Islam in word and action. This is the essence of being a Muslim and children will learn the spirit of Islam directly from you, their role model, not just as a collection of rituals but as the highest state that a person can reach.
- Maintain a cordial relationship with all our neighbours. This will create social skills in the child and a tendency to help others in

need. This *khidmah* aspect of Islam is in the Prophetic *Sunnah* and a major ingredient of a happy and successful society.

- Arrange regular family sessions. They help bonding among family members and increase knowledge of and conviction in Islam. We should encourage our children in the affairs of the family through engagement in discussion of family issues.
- Avoid passing on the stress of our job or of our lives to the children. There is no doubt that modern life is stressful, but younger children are not in a position to appreciate that. It may lower us in their eyes when we unload our frustrations on our children.
- Keep family arguments away from the children. Parents must show the utmost tolerance and sensitivity among themselves. There may be arguments among adults in the family, but children should not be overburdened with them before they are in a position to understand them.

Chapter Five

Secondary School Years

The seeking of knowledge is obligatory for every Muslim.
(At-Tirmidhi)

Choosing a Secondary School

Making the right choice of secondary school is one of the most important decisions for children and a daunting one for parents. After the security of the primary years, the transition to secondary school is a time of anxiety and uncertainty. However, most children take it as an exciting experience in their lives. Secondary schools are different from primary ones, in terms of size, environment, teaching style and pastoral demand. They offer specialist curricula in subjects like art and design, technology and modern languages. Unlike primary schools, curriculum subjects in secondary schools are taught by subject teachers. This puts extra demands on children to learn faster. Instead of working in one classroom with one teacher, they move across the school to different subject rooms to experience the tuition of various teachers.

While primary school gives children a solid foundation in their education, secondary school prepares them for their role in society, with more rigorous tests which may count towards their academic careers. Bearing in mind the importance of a good secondary education, conscientious parents wish to choose the best possible school for their children. Some parents even move to a different area to have access to a better school if they are convinced that schools in their locality are not of a high enough standard.

Choosing a good school can be very difficult for Muslim parents as we must look both for academic excellence and good moral and social environment. Fulfilling multiple demands is almost impossible. Parents need to consider the distance their child must travel to get to school and prepare them for any admissions tests. Private or selective schools are usually single-sex and parents can be assured of a high academic standard there. These are available not only to those who are financially able to fund their children's fees but also to exceptionally bright pupils who can gain scholarships and bursaries. State or non-selective schools are the main option for most parents and can vary widely in their academic and other performance, so parents need to be informed about the decision that they make.

Secondary schools generally publish a prospectus in which they show how their school is performing academically, with figures on examination passes and attendance rates. They also arrange for open days or evenings for parents so that they can learn first-hand how the school operates. Primary schools provide valuable information about local secondary schools. Parents can learn about the ethos and attitudes of a particular school through visiting and talking to present pupils, teachers and other parents. There are choices available and Muslim parents need to take advice from others if necessary. The choice has to be made wisely and in good time.

Good schools are those with an emphasis on academic progress, strong discipline, a prompt start to lessons and a good relationship between teachers and pupils. Every child is unique and the key is to place a child within an environment that suits them. A studious child will flourish in a school that emphasises academic achievement, but a less academically inclined pupil may thrive in a school that offers more non-academic subjects and facilities. What makes secondary education an enjoyable learning process is its inclusive nature, positive ethos and the interest shown in the children. Good schools cater for all types of pupils so that the talented do not become bored and frustrated and, at the same time, under-achievers do not feel left out.

It is important that parents are armed with full and correct information, so that they can make an informed choice about a secondary school. The following checklist, though not exhaustive, may prove helpful in this regard:

» What is the catchment area like? Is the area safe and socially stable?

» What does the latest inspection report say about the school?

» Is the school mixed or single-sex?

» What extra-curricular facilities does it have?

» What is the level of academic achievement of the school?

» Where do the pupils normally go when they finish school?

» Is bullying a concern in the school and how do staff deal with it?

» Does it have a written behaviour policy and is it followed rigorously?

» Are parents welcome in the school and can they meet teachers easily?

» What is the absence rate? How does the school deal with non-authorised absences?

» What are the fixed-term (occasional) and permanent exclusion rates?

» What are the children's and parents' attitudes towards the school?
» What is the relationship between the teachers and children like?
» What is the behaviour of the children like with each other?
» What is the homework policy of the school?
» What special needs facilities does the school offer, if needed?
» Is the school tidy and clean and does it offer a friendly learning environment?

A Single-sex or Mixed School?

There are two opposing views about the issue of single-sex schooling. Proponents of co-education believe that boys and girls should grow up and learn about life together, so that they know each other well. Free mixing is encouraged as a progressive and liberal idea and anyone not conforming to this idea is considered out-dated. Their idea of gender role is competitive, not complementary. Men and women are generally not valued according to specific strengths and weaknesses.

In contrast, there are some who feel a woman's place is in the home or more specifically in the kitchen, only to cook for and serve other family members. Not only do they see the education of females as a waste of time, they believe it to be detrimental to society. In the name of religion and culture, many women lose their natural human right to get an education.

Islam treads a middle way. Education is vital in Islam, and seeking knowledge is obligatory for both males and females. Both girls and boys should be educated in a setting that helps them to achieve their full potential.

From a purely educational point of view, many Western researchers have found that boys and girls both perform better in single-sex schools. Irrespective of religious and social views, they recommend single-sex schooling for better educational achievement. As a result of these research findings, and of course due to parental demand, some mixed schools even arrange separate single-sex tutorial groups and recreation time for better learning and discipline. This research is borne out by the statistics that girls perform better at national exam level in girls' only schools.

Boys and girls are biologically and emotionally different. Boys, and particularly pubescent boys, can be quite aggressive in their behaviour and may demand more attention from teachers. Girls, who are quieter by nature, will lose out in a mixed environment. Boys and girls mature at different rates and they tend to have somewhat different educational interests. Arguably single-sex schools cater best for the needs of their pupils and have a greater specific understanding of their problems and issues.

From a religious point of view, Islam requires that young men and women maintain the purity of their sexual lives from the very beginning of their pubescent life. This not only means that they should not indulge in a sexual relationship before marriage but also in any behaviour that may lead to it, however seemingly harmless in itself, such as flirting or lustful eye contact. This is more easily done in a single-sex environment where the temptation simply does not exist and children can focus on the purpose for which they are at school. This does not mean pubescent boys and girls should be totally segregated in social life, but that these occasions are within the bounds of Islamic law.

Muslim Denominational Schools[8]

Even single-sex schools in a libertine environment are not without their problems. The permissive ethos in society is reflected within the school gates and Muslim children can be left feeling confused between the value-rich environment at home and the more amoral one at school. It is for this reason that many Muslim parents may feel their child will flourish and be more confident in a faith school, where home and school values complement each other more closely and create less confusion in children.

The aim of a faith school is to teach pupils the same mainstream syllabus (with the addition of subjects such as Arabic and Islam) while instilling universal and inclusive Islamic values, so that Muslim children can comfortably relate to the wider society with confidence and contribute to its progress.

Critics point out that faith schools encourage segregation and ghetto culture and that children should be educated in an environment that is reflective of wider society. However, the concept of separate schooling was not invented by Muslims. Over the centuries, a great number of educational institutions have been selective based on social class (private schools), religion (religious denominational) and ability (grammar schools). The history of all-inclusive comprehensive education is fairly recent and it is telling that it has not led to the abolition of the above mentioned schools.

Some religious denominational schools may show a degree of insularity, but as a whole, faith schools should be seen in the broader social context. Minority communities struggling to maintain their traditions need confidence and security in their early stages as they do not always start from the same level playing field. Once children

---

8 The Muslim Parent's Handbook: What Every Muslim Parent Should Know, Shabbir Akhtar, Ta-Ha Publishers, London, 1993 (out of print)
Muslim Demands for Their Own Denominational Schools in the UK, M. A. Bari, Muslim Education Quarterly, The Islamic Academy, Cambridge, Vol. 10, No. 2, 1993

are well-anchored in their own religious and cultural traditions and confident within themselves, they not only survive but contribute fully in a pluralist society. Natural interaction then leads to wholesome positive integration based on mutual respect rather than the minority community being forced to conform.

Muslims should play a positive and effective role in educating their children within Islam and within the confines of a pluralist society. They should value the importance of inclusive education in a wide sense, promote equality and encourage creativity. In other words, they must not fail themselves. Whether parents feel that is best done in a faith school or in a mainstream school is their choice.

Preparing a Solid Foundation for Life

The selection of a good school does not signal the end of the parental input in their child's education. Parents need to be vigilant with their children in the following areas and make sure that they are getting the best out of their school years.

Academic Achievement

It is widely acknowledged that good literacy, numeracy, IT and communication skills put people at an advantage. Without these skills children would find it difficult to grasp the wider curriculum and soon lose their self-esteem. As they grow older some may lose their self-confidence and by the time they leave school they may start feeling that the world is not welcoming to them in terms of the job market and social recognition. Some of them may even end up becoming a burden on society. It is the responsibility of both the school and parents to ensure that their children do not 'fall through the net', but it is parents who need to be more careful in this regard.

Caring and responsible parents ask their children how their day was, what they did, what homework they have received. It is important that parents are aware of who their friends are, how they are doing in class, which subjects they find enjoyable and which ones they find more challenging. Communicating frankly and in a friendly manner can help to identify any potential issues or problems before they escalate.

It does not matter if parents are not directly able to help their children in academic subjects; in fact many parents cannot, but children must feel that their parents care about their educational achievements and their day-to-day life. Parents need to look out for the following:

» Does the child go to school willingly?
» Are they facing any problems with their class/homework?
» Are they getting on well at school?
» Do they come home straight away after school?
» Are they happy every day or do they suddenly become quiet?
» Are they getting on well socially?
» Are their grades/marks consistent?

Children need a good routine and a balanced timetable for their study at home and can even be encouraged to make their own so that they feel comfortable following it. There should be two timetables, however informal; one for school days and the other for weekends and holidays. Both parents and children should try to follow these with some seriousness and consistence. The routine should cater for the following:

» Subject study and homework (more in the weekdays)
» Socialisation with friends (more in the holidays)
» Free time or personal space (every day, but more in the holidays)
» Using computers for knowledge and schoolwork (as and when necessary)

» Arabic learning and Qur'an recitation (every day, but more in the holidays)
» Youth activities, e.g., games/sports, in mosques or reliable youth centres (more in the holidays)
» Newspaper reading, watching TV for news and innocent entertainment (regularly)

Homework and coursework form increasingly more important components of school education as children progress through the years. They show how children work independently with the help of additional texts or information from other sources, such as reference books, the internet, newspapers and other media. Parents should ensure that they allow children the time and space to do this well. This means that the home environment should be quiet and that there should be a place for each child to do their work in a comfortable and studious setting. Many schools have homework clubs for pupils who otherwise find difficulty in completing it at home. Parents need to encourage their children to do homework or coursework on their own, even if they can help them directly, so that they become self-reliant. If parents feel it is necessary, extra tutoring can be arranged for some subjects.

In order to achieve good grades and succeed academically, children have to acquire the necessary learning skills, which will be of use to them throughout their life as learning is a life-long endeavour. Individual learners, depending on their interests and capabilities, can maximise their learning through a combination of the following skills:

» Rote learning: There is generally no cognitive demand in this learning and it has little context. It is important for memorising some text, such as, remembering quotations, formulas and references.

» Factual learning: There is little cognitive demand in this learning, but it provides context. It is important for very relevant, down-to-earth learning, such as scientific facts.

» Conceptual or abstract learning: There is cognitive demand in this learning but it has little context. This is important in art and some other subject areas.

» Critical learning: This has cognitive demand and context. It is important for any creative subject, such as poetry and literature.

Learning is most effective when the child understands why they are studying the subject, how it fits in with the world around them and engage in using their intellect. The *du'a* 'My Lord, increase me in knowledge' (Surah Ta-Ha 20:114) is a useful one to bear in mind.

Exams are, of course, important in formal education and this can be a worrying and stressful time for children, particularly national level exams. Parental support and love is vital. Parents need to encourage their children to prepare well for all exams and help them in making and following a routine before and during the exam period. Closer to exams, parents need to be more considerate and they should step back from socialising so that children have the opportunity to study without any interruption of going out or having guests in the house. It is counter-productive to put excess pressure on children to achieve certain grades. Exercise, leisure and rest should be incorporated in any exam preparation timetable, so that children can perform to the best of their ability when exams approach. Being exhausted through too many sleepless nights is not a good idea.

Other Talents

Human beings are complex and highly intelligent creatures and there are different types of intelligence[9]:

- » Personal intelligence - makes one aware of oneself, one's thoughts and needs.
- » Physical intelligence - helps one to learn through the body and develop physical skills.
- » Emotional intelligence - makes one aware of others and relating well to them.
- » Visual intelligence - helps one learn through seeing and being aware of shapes and space.
- » Linguistic intelligence - helps one to learn, speak, read and write through language.
- » Mathematical intelligence - helps one to understand numbers and become logical in thinking.
- » Scientific intelligence - helps one to learn about the world and being curious to find out more.
- » Musical intelligence - helps one to learn through listening and being aware of sounds.
- » Philosophical intelligence - makes one think and ask questions about the meaning of life.

Children are born with some of these aspects of intelligence, and some may be gifted with a particular one in abundance. Academic institutions can only measure and test some of the more traditional forms of intelligence. Those children that are gifted in these areas are likely to do well at school. However, those who struggle with traditional measures of intelligence may be intelligent in other areas. For example, a child who finds maths and science hard may be a very empathetic and soft-hearted person who engages well with other people. Parents

9 Head Start - How to develop your child's mind, Robert Fisher, Souvenir Press Ltd, London, 1999

and teachers need to explore this in their children and help them find out the skills in which they excel and provide extra support for those in which they do not.

Physical and Mental Fitness

A happy life depends on balanced physical, emotional and mental growth. Parents need to provide their children with a nutritious, wholesome and moderate diet to support this period of growth that they are undergoing. In addition, regular exercise and a relatively stress-free life will help them to stay fit and healthy. It is all too easy nowadays for children to sit in front of TV or computers for hours. In addition to making children physically inactive, it can make them dull, socially passive and unable to interact with other people.

Another faculty which Islam encourages us to develop is that of thinking and reflecting. Children should be given adequate freedom, but necessary guidance, to cultivate their:

> » Information processing skills;
> » Reasoning skills;
> » Enquiry skills;
> » Creative thinking;
> » Evaluation skills.

Both teachers and parents need to encourage their young people to think and ensure that the school years do not just become an exercise in committing endless facts to memory that are promptly forgotten when the exams end. When the power of thinking is inhibited, the mind becomes stagnant and does not stir and move forward. The success of early Muslims lay in this creative engagement of their brain in advancing the frontiers of human endeavour. The sky was their limit. Islam linked this power of thinking with self-awareness and a sense of responsibility to other creatures, but through the knowledge of accountability to

Allah. As a result, Muslims succeeded in creating a knowledge-based civilisation for the benefit of all. It was rich in creativity and action but, at the same time, deep in spirituality. The European Renaissance was also a period rich in creativity and full of dynamism, but it sadly de-linked human beings from accountability to our Creator. It structured human life with individual self-fulfilment and national interest. Europe thus became lost in the wilderness of secular materialism.

Personal, Social and Life Skills

A good education is needed for success in life. But education is not simply about collecting good grades in school and good degrees at university. Parents need to provide young people with the opportunity to develop and explore their talents and interests, engaging in jobs or careers that interest them and lead them to work for the benefit of humanity. The Muslim *ummah* needs people of knowledge and understanding who can challenge the stagnation and apathy of the past few hundred years.

The struggle for children to achieve academic excellence should be accompanied equally by an effort to realise their personal, social, intellectual and spiritual potential. Learning to become responsible and gradually independent in life receives a new impetus in secondary school. Tools such as voluntary work, outings and extra-curricular activities are all helpful in disseminating these skills and parents should encourage their children to actively participate in them. This will help them in becoming full and active members of society.

Personal skills are about understanding oneself and one's self-worth with a view to attaining self-control and behaving in a dignified manner. Maxims such as, 'know thyself' or 'those who know themselves, know their Lord' have guided human beings through the ages in exploring their selves, although certainly the latter leads beyond the self and to knowledge of the Creator. This helps one to become more mindful and conscious without becoming self-centred or arrogant. How children perceive themselves and what they think of their appearance, personality and talents are important for their balanced growth. These give them self-respect and self-confidence. Parental guidelines can save children from the pitfalls of over-confidence or low self-esteem. We should talk about this with our children and involve them in such projects from which they learn how to reflect on and evaluate their achievements and shortcomings and identify ways to deal with them. Conscious awareness of one's responsibility is a key to success.

Social skills are about understanding others and acting wisely in human relationships. Children naturally learn this through their own relationships with their parents and others around them and also through observing their parents' relationships with others. Human beings are a social species. 'People skills' or the ability to form good relationships with others is at the heart of social life. This can be done through talking with others, showing them respect with good manners, showing sensitivity to and empathy with others and working together. Social skills help children make friends, recognise differing values and live together peacefully.

Life skills are about acquiring the know-how of living decently, without being irritating to or a burden on others. All these skills can be learned by children through conscious effort as well as the benefit of parental experience.

Spiritual Attainment

The modern world has unfortunately become spiritually barren and the result is anxiety, disquiet, stress and tension which pervade the human mind today. Peace and tranquillity are all but lost due to neglect of the soul. It is an irony that overwhelming materialism has reduced us into 'intelligent animals' with little left for our spirits. People nowadays take great pride in their spectacular material progress. The 'mini gods' of whims, desires, technology, art and the like have occupied our lives. Consequently, we are suffering from a terrible spiritual thirst and many are now turning to a variety of different means to quench it.

Human beings' creation, survival and success are absolutely dependent on Allah, our Creator. He has given us freedom so that when we return back to Him on the Day of Judgement, we can give full account of our deeds on earth. Firm belief in this is at the root of spirituality. However, Muslims never make a show of spirituality, nor do they become fatalist. As spirituality flourishes within us, it becomes embedded in our nature and reflected in our appearance, expression and, in fact, the whole being. The spiritual height of the Companions of the Prophet ﷺ is mentioned in the Qur'an: 'Their mark is on their faces, the traces of prostration' (Surah al-Fath 48:29).

In the midst of a spiritual desert, Muslim parents have an obligation to create an oasis for their children and equip them with love and loyalty to Allah and His Messenger ﷺ. Spiritual attainment brings peace and tranquillity. It is true that the challenge to inculcate deep love for Allah in children in these modern times is daunting, but children by nature, are adventurous and explorative. If they are properly guided into the world of infinite joy in spiritual solace, they will embrace it themselves.

Secondary Challenges

Once the hurdle of gaining admission into a secondary school has been cleared, a new phase of parenting begins. At the start of the school year, there are natural concerns as to how children will settle into the new school environment, the first few months of which are crucial. Children are normally quick to make new friends and, depending on the school environment, they soon fit into the system.

However, this may not be a smooth process for some, especially in schools that have pupils of diverse ethnic and cultural backgrounds. Pro-active and assertive children easily take their position in the new setup, but quiet, lonely and shy children may take time. Some, especially those who are too dependent on their parents, may face difficulties in adjusting, as teachers generally expect secondary children to be more independent. Parents, school and the children themselves all have to play their part in positively integrating such children in the school. The challenges are many: educational, social and, of course, very much related with the world of adolescence.

Practising Islam at School

Post-pubescent young Muslims have an obligation to follow the compulsory Islamic rites and abide by Islamic principles. This is a big test for secondary school age children, who need to observe their essential religious practices in school hours. They will need to perform their *salah* at school on a daily basis and observe fasting (*sawm*) throughout the month of Ramadan. In addition, girls may need to make adjustments to their school uniform to allow them to dress modestly, including wearing the headscarf. During sports lessons, both boys and girls need to be aware that their *awrah* is covered.

Schools in most Western countries are generally accommodating of the religious rights of minorities and head teachers generally comply with religious requests from Muslim students. This is in tune with the equal opportunities policy that accommodates racial and religious diversity. There may be some strong secularist head teachers who can either procrastinate or refuse to provide this basic need to Muslim children, but their number is small.

Should that be the case, Muslim boys and girls are in a unique position to argue the case of their civil and religious rights with head teachers and, in that process, many of the misunderstandings can be removed. What matters in this endeavour is their conviction to Islam, their courteous manners and articulate persuasiveness. Islam is strong on its basic principles, but there is no room for hot-headedness in argument. It is also important to understand that there is plenty of room for flexibility in secondary aspects of Islam. Muslim children have reason to be proud of their *deen* and enthusiastic about it and they should have the support of their parents to do so.

Bullying and the Broader Issue of Safety

Bullying in schools is a major issue that costs society in many ways. Bullying means deliberately hurting someone, often repeatedly over a period of time, when the victims are unable for whatever reason or find it difficult to defend themselves. The scourge of bullying can take the following forms:

» Physical - hitting, kicking, taking belongings;
» Verbal - name calling, and insulting and offensive remarks;
» Indirect - spreading nasty stories, excluding others from social groups, making a child the subject of malicious remarks.

A student can be bullied because of his/her differences from others, based on any of the six diversity strands – race, gender, disability, sexual orientation, age and religion. Stories of pupils physically and mentally traumatised by bullying are sadly common in many schools. The fear of bullying is experienced by a significant section of the student population, particularly first year pupils in secondary schools. Good schools have strong anti-bullying policies and monitoring mechanisms. Schools consistently showing zero tolerance to bullying, succeed in creating an ethos of mutual understanding and respect. However, success depends on every member of the school community, including the victims themselves.

A bully generally targets someone who is seen to be isolated, vulnerable and docile. Muslim children can be picked on for their ethnic and cultural features. Muslim girls who wear headscarves can be targeted. Parents should take extra care to educate their children on how to confront bullying. Parents should encourage their children to make friends, interact with others, become assertive and challenging if they encounter a bully, but never to resort to abuse or violence or counteract bullying with bullying.

Discipline

The desire for freedom is inherent in human nature. As children grow and step into secondary schools, they start to gain a taste of freedom. They travel by themselves, organise their own work and, in many cases, are allowed to go out of school during lunch time. This freedom and space breeds creativity, innovation, enterprise and motivation in them. On the other hand, too much personal freedom can give rise to a selfish 'couldn't care less' attitude which erodes family structure and the fabric of society. Freedom without responsibility is dangerous. For any civilised society they are intertwined. Freedom brings choice, but one has to learn the consequences of choice. In Islam, accountability to the Creator, one's own self and others are the perimeters of freedom. This may seem inhibiting to some, but it makes freedom meaningful and saves human beings from chaos. Without any boundaries on freedom, there is social anarchy.

The unlicensed and quite illusory freedom in society filters down and impacts on school life. Class discipline is now the most difficult aspect of teaching in many secondary schools. Some teachers leave their profession because of the stress caused by children who give little respect to teachers or the system. Fear of the chaos in classrooms is also causing concern over teacher recruitment. Teachers in many inner-city schools are, in effect, engaged in 'child-minding', instead of teaching the curriculum. A significant proportion of teachers seek advice on stress management from their unions and help-lines. This generally becomes worse in mixed schools where many upper school boys and girls behave openly in an unbecoming manner, not only in the corridors or in the corners of the playground, but sometimes in classrooms as well.

Schools are not isolated islands in a society. Young people's lives are dictated by wider social norms, such as TV programmes, internet, printed media, parental lifestyles and other factors. The challenges young people face in their lives are multi-faceted:

» Personal Factors - low self-esteem, learning difficulties, emotional and behavioural difficulties.

» Family Influences - poor parenting, economic deprivation, family conflicts.

» School Environments - the curriculum, peer pressure, the hidden curriculum, low teacher expectation.

» Social Factors - race and culture, social deprivation, unemployment, media imagery.

» Social Trends - moral permissiveness, sexual promiscuity and the ideological maze.

Like everyone in society, young people at school look for recognition and a sense of worth. Those who are disadvantaged and feel strongly so, often tend to express themselves in unconventional ways. Gang-fights, drug abuse and petty crimes are some of the outlets and anti-social practices they adopt to vent their frustration and anger against the system. With negative role models abounding, many of them follow social trends that clash with the interests of society at large. New technological gadgets, with their value-less promotions, often make them the worse tools of self-indulgence.

Young people always want to feel special. They crave to be recognised and noticed. They want to be at the forefront of any social change. An example of this is the recent explosion in mobile phone use that has enabled young people to show their worth at school. Surveys have shown that mobile phone use has become a symbol of dignity and, like many other trends, has become a part of youth culture. Is youth culture entirely a creation of marketing bosses intent on selling gadgets and consumer items? This is a live discussion of our time.

Given this laxity in youth culture, can Muslim parents afford to take a back seat in the affairs of their children, especially in their transition to adulthood?

In the first place, when making the decision about secondary schools, parents need to look at the discipline policy of a school and the general behaviour of its pupils as they spill out of the school gates. This must assume as much importance as academic performance, as a child cannot learn effectively if they do not have a disciplined structure within which to work.

Secondly, Muslim parents must create an environment at home and within the community that creates some structure and a sense of discipline and responsibility with clear boundaries which should not be overstepped by children. This cannot be achieved by simply resorting to 'additional' Qur'an or community language teaching at home or in the mosque at the weekend or after school. When Muslim parents are able to create a positive and disciplined environment in their homes, on the street, in mosques and community centres, then discipline becomes embedded in the nature of young children. These children then grow to be active rather than reactive, positive rather than pessimistic and collaborative rather than individualistic. They try hard to create a decent environment in their schools as well.

Discipline comes about in children when they see their parents and others in the community disciplined; praying on time, keeping their promises, being respectful to others. It comes about when parents explain what the boundaries of good and acceptable behaviour are, when they are consistent about taking a child to task who has overstepped those boundaries and when they themselves are exemplary about keeping well within those boundaries. This requires parents to deal with clarity, integrity and justice and in unison with one another. Children must never be shamed, humiliated or degraded especially in front of others.

Parents have to keep in mind that coercion does not help in implementing discipline. Forced discipline often brings a negative outcome, despite good intentions. Young people, especially in free societies, want to know the reason for any action. Too much control with only do's and don'ts leads at best to docility and passivity and at worst rebellion. In order to be effective in discipline, parents must avoid unnecessary confrontations with children. The following points are a guide for effective disciplining:

» Understand the psychology of the child in order to deal with them effectively. Simple observation and common sense are needed.

» Use moderation in behaviour towards children. Too much liberty may spoil them, while too much rigidity may make them rebellious. Islam teaches moderation in life and children should not grow up in extremes.

» Ignore their mistakes and give them space. Adolescents do make mistakes and this is how they learn, but they need space to get rid of their embarrassment, anger, depression and frustration. Parents must learn to discern when to be there for their children and when to leave them alone.

» Avoid making negative comments, even for fun, about children's choice, behaviour and actions. These have been shown to be demoralising to young people.

» Avoid using language such as 'Never do this!' Instead use words like 'I would be happier if you didn't do it this or that way.'

» Empathise with children. Avoid repeating behaviour or comments that hurt them. Children are under tremendous pressure nowadays and we need to understand their perspectives.

» Discipline them with justice. Disciplining secondary school children requires sensitivity. While they must be disciplined for any wrongdoing, they should not be shamed, especially in front of younger siblings. Justice must be maintained and both parents should be involved in the process.

» Avoid scolding children in front of their friends. Should any problem arise, parents should deal with it privately and later on when the situation calms down.

» Parents should be consistent in their mood and their discipline so as to create a clear impression of what is right and wrong, otherwise teenagers may feel confused and start thinking that erratic behaviour is normal.

Sex and Sexuality Education

Muslim children attending mixed secondary schools undergo some psychological and social pressure from their peers and, unless reared within a proper Islamic environment, may end up giving in to a self-indulgent lifestyle. Parents and the community should adopt a multi-pronged safeguard mechanism in order to help children navigate their way out from the danger of pre-marital sex. Children need to be strengthened with Islamic knowledge and taqwa so that they can stand firm when faced with temptation. They need to be given a decent alternative environment in which to channel their youthful energy. Young Muslims need to be reminded of the exemplary life of Yusuf ﷺ, who although was lured by pretty women around him was more inclined to the love of his Lord and preferred prison to sexual indulgence.

Because of the rise of teenage pregnancy in modern society, schools offer sex education from as early as the primary years. In secondary schools this is done in personal/social/health lessons and science lessons, with the former covering the human aspect of adult relationships and safe sex practices and science covering physical details of pubescent changes and reproduction. Parents should be aware of what their child's school offers in the way of such education and at what age their child is introduced to what information. It is possible for parents to withdraw their child from some sex education lessons, but they need to work with the school on this. However, it is important parents familiarise themselves with the basic biological facts of puberty and reproduction and discuss these with their own children in a decent and sensitive manner. Islam promotes courtesy in the behaviour between a man and woman. This is all the more important with young people who are naturally driven by impulsive passion in their early and not-so-mature adolescent lives. A sense of respect for each other, responsibility in life and accountability to Allah are the guiding principles when young males and females need to deal with each other. Islam requires chastity from its adherents and Muslim children must learn this from childhood. Islam teaches us to remain vigilant and keep away from physical proximity, intimate closeness and physical contact among post-puberty boys and girls, that may tempt them into a physical relationship later on.

Parents must be open about this issue with their children. Within the limits of decency and in all sincerity, they should discuss the Islamic requirements of a wholesome approach towards dealing with the opposite sex. They need to take the lead in teaching their children about the roles and responsibilities of men and women before school, TV and others in society do this. It would be impractical to advise young people to remain aloof from the opposite sex. What they need is guidance in self-control to attain spiritual heights despite their surroundings. In-built *taqwa* (consciousness of the presence of Allah and the resulting avoidance of wrong action and engagement in right action) is the only way to sail through this difficult period.

In the same way, parents need to discuss the sensitive issues of sexual orientation and same sex-relationships with their children at the appropriate age.

The Issue of Identity[10]

Children begin to develop more awareness of their identity in secondary school when their horizon starts to broaden. As they grow in physical and intellectual maturity, they gradually come to terms with their own background, family and community roots. Depending on their upbringing, they start seeing the world through their own eyes. The dream life of childhood gradually disappears and they learn how to confront a real world of religious, cultural and ethnic differences. Where do they fit in that world? How do they relate to their friends from other communities, who may possess very different attitudes towards life? One thing Muslim parents must guard against is their children growing up with insular and selfish attitudes. Muslims are a community of purpose for a common good, so by nature they should be sociable, hospitable, helpful and open-minded. The essence of Islam is to serve humanity and it is not part of the spirit of Islam to shut oneself away or not care for others.

Identity is multi-faceted and all faces are essential in a person's life. Religious, national, geographic and other identities give the wider

---

10 Identity is a hotly debated issue in Britain. Prominent politicians often raise this issue and attract media headlines. Unfortunately, once again, Muslim youth are often asked certain questions on this in a way others are not. The subject is discussed from a holistic viewpoint in the author's book *Race, Religion and Muslim Identity in Britain*, Awakening Publishers, 2005, UK

picture of a person. Unfortunately, Islamic or even religious identity in post-modern societies is viewed negatively by intolerant secularists nowadays and young Muslim men are often perceived negatively if they are seen to be 'religious'. There is a great deal of ignorance about religion in general and Islam in particular within the public at large. Muslim children can experience negative stereotyping from schools, the media and in day-to-day life. As such, many of them may feel vulnerable. Some even feel embarrassed to identify themselves as Muslims. This social stigma has led some young Muslims to live double lives. Some, although small in number, even alter their names or accept their alteration by teachers or their peer group in order to feel accepted. This simply lowers their self-esteem further.

Muslim parents must always observe their children to see whether their young ones are keeping well and developing their self-confidence. In a world generally antagonistic to Muslims and Islam, Muslim children may develop despondency and fatalism in their life. It is imperative that parents become extra caring towards their children, empathise with them and share some of their burden, so that they grow with a 'self at rest and at peace' (Surah al-Fajr 89:28).

Muslim parents thus have an immense responsibility in the current world environment to educate their adolescents to be proud of their multiple identities. They have to assure them that being a Muslim does not exclude them from being British or Asian or American, not only theoretically but also in reality. Multiple identities are rather an asset, as they manifest the mosaic nature of human diversity and should thus be celebrated. They enrich a society in all aspects, provided the spirit of human dignity and equality of opportunity are maintained by all. In a society where freedom of religious practice and freedom of expression are enshrined by law, a confident Muslim's multiple identity enhances positive social integration. Muslim parents have the added task of educating their adolescent children that their 'Muslimness' demands from them a proactive engagement with others in order to play their civic role and social responsibility for common good.

The Black-hole of the 'Pastime'

The modern entertainment industry is rich, powerful and employs a huge number of people. With Hollywood and Disney's vast empire, they are taking over children's imaginations, and also their free time. The films produced by these companies, often find a way of entertaining children whatever the time of day. Action thrillers and romances, all manage to lure these susceptible and vulnerable children into spending their (and their parents') money on watching them, buying them, and also buying their associated merchandise. Children think that if they don't watch the major celebrities, people will think that there is something wrong with them and in school they may be 'outcast'.

It is not only the Western entertainment industry that grabs young people's attention; the Eastern amusement industry also plays a major part in the lives of young Asians everywhere. With Bollywood producing hundreds of films a year, it is difficult for young Asians to keep away from modern 'Eastern', mythology-tinted, Indian entertainment. To many Muslims of Eastern origin this is probably worse as the characters bear some similarity to their own lives; some Indian film stars are idolised by many Asian youngsters, including Muslims.

It is not only films that fill up young children's timetables, but computers, mobiles, video games and TV also manage to pull young people into the black hole of 'passing time'. PlayStations, Gamecubes and X-Box's now grace living rooms, taking away their free time and engaging their brains in fantasies. The computer-generated virtual world becomes their reality and many children fail to comprehend the complexities of real life. Even the concepts of life and death lose seriousness in their virtual reality. What is the effect of this? Research has shown that TV, video- and computer games make children more aggressive, even violent.

And then there is the music industry that seduces the ear and mind. Often sexually explicit, the meaningless message of the music engages the whole personalities of our young people. It is true that human beings need some sort of music, but what type?

Music is a part of human culture. It is as old as human beings themselves. Music has the power to speak, arouse feeling and passion. Mothers sing their children to sleep, armies march to the sound of drums and other creatures sing to express their happiness and to praise Allah. The melodious recitation of the Qur'an can create feelings of devotion, joy and anxiety among believers. All children respond naturally to rhythm and melody. There are an increasing number of non-instrumental music with positive lyrics that praise Allah and His creation in the form of *nasheeds*.

Islam is not meant to be a dry and monotonous religion. It has enjoyment and entertainment refreshing to the human heart. Muslims have never lacked for lighter moments and uplifting experiences: 'Entertain the hearts in between hours, for if the hearts get tired they become blind' (Sunan ad-Daylami).

Can Muslim parents insulate their children from these pastimes? In reality, we cannot. We cannot ignore the demands from our youngsters to buy something for their amusement, even if we prefer not to, because otherwise our children would be left out among their friends at school. However, parents must use their judgement on what to buy and set some rules regarding their use. This may sound compromising to some Muslims, but it is a fundamental insight of Islam that when faced with two ills, we must choose the lesser of the two.

Chapter Six

Into the World of Responsibility

The feet of the Children of Adam, on the Day of Judgement, will not move from their Lord until being asked five things: His life and how it occupied him, his youth and what he did while it lasted, his wealth, how he acquired it and how he spent it, his knowledge and what he did with it. (At-Tirmidhi)

Parents will Always be Parents

It is a universal truth that parents have great ambitions for their children and try to provide for them the things that they did not have themselves. Even the Prophets and sages did not step back once their children left adolescence but guided them when they became adults. Of course, as adults, people take responsibility for their own life but as Muslims we owe each other good counsel for as long as we are alive. In a positive family environment, elderly parents do not feel inhibited in advising their grown-up children due to the family bond, which has made Muslim society strongly inclusive and in turn contributed to a humane Muslim civilisation in the past. In return for the love, protection and wisdom offered by parents to their children, parents naturally feel looked after, valued and supplicated for in their old age.

In the Qur'an, Luqman, a pre-Islamic sage, counselled his son regarding pure *tawhid* and about his duties (Surah Luqman 31:13-19). In the same manner, when Ibrahim ﷺ found that the wife of his beloved son, Isma'il ﷺ, failed to pass the test of gratitude, he advised his son to release her from marriage and find a better one. Isma'il ﷺ dutifully carried out his father's counsel. This account is narrated by 'Abdullah ibn 'Abbas ﷺ in a long *hadith* in Sahih al-Bukhari.

History has also recorded the motherly counsel of Asma bint Abi Bakr ﷺ who, in her very old age, encouraged her son, the famous 'Abdullah ibn az-Zubayr ﷺ not to waver in his fight against the tyrant Hajjaj ibn Yusuf. When she heard that 'Abdullah was distressed about the possible mutilation of his body after his imminent martyrdom, she tenderly rebuked him not to worry so much about what could happen to his dead body.

These stories carry a significant message about the role of Muslim parents in Islam. A parent's legal duty may be complete when a child crosses puberty, but their concern never ends. The seed of a loving relationship is sown in childhood and keeps bearing fruit until parents complete their journey on earth. Allah has elevated parents in the eyes of children because of all they have done for them and because of the natural maturity and experience they have acquired during the course of their long life. However, wise parents never arbitrarily use or abuse their privileged position to make unjustified demands on their children or interfere in their lives. Our job is to offer unbiased advice that is in the best interest of our children. It is up to them whether or not they take it.

Guidance in Career Choice

Young people are faced with a multitude of choices regarding further education and careers. Should they go to university? What degree should they do? What profession should they choose? Informed parents can guide their children directly in these crucial decisions with the help of school career's services and work experience/ placement opportunities.

Education after sixteen is not statutory; it depends on each child's interest, ambition and now increasingly financial considerations. Less academically inclined youngsters may choose to enter into the workplace and start gaining practical experience and work their way up the hierarchy through hard work and on-the-job training. Others may wish to take up a vocational course that is less rigorous academically but provides further training in the relevant practical skills. There is a great deal of choice as to how these can be pursued - at schools, colleges, full-time, part-time, even distance learning courses - so those who do wish to continue their studies have a number of options that can fit in with their constraints or lifestyle. For the more academically inclined there is the option to complete school and follow onto university.

Education after sixteen has its own challenges. As children grow up and learn to take responsibility for their lives, they start enjoying more freedom. Educational institutions rely on self-initiative in students. Parents also expect that they can relax somewhat and they look forward to more independent but responsible offspring.

Success, according to Islam, is two-fold – success in this world and the Hereafter. So, the key to success is in earning a *halal* income in a dignified manner through hard work. Successful parents are those who infuse in their children the strength of *iman* that makes no compromise with forbidden earning, no matter what the temptation is. They guide their children in self-exploration so that their potential is harnessed to the full. Young Muslims may choose to be business people, teachers, electricians, social workers or any profession that suits them, but they should never lose sight of their focus in serving Allah by serving the community and the wider society.

Some parents can be insistent on their children choosing certain professions. They may have long harboured ambitions for their son or daughter to be, say, a doctor or lawyer. While giving an opinion or mild persuasion is fine, it is never wise to force children to do anything. Children are not there to fulfil the desires or regrets that their parents may have had in their own past lives and parents should try not to re-live their lives through their children. The Muslim *ummah* needs quality people in all areas of life, from Astronomy to Zoology. We have today an imbalance in subject choice among Muslims with less interest in creative and social sciences that needs to be redressed.

University: The Frontier of Knowledge

Education is the backbone of a people. University education has the potential of opening the frontiers of knowledge in a challenging world. Muslim youth should be encouraged to take up the challenge if they have the ability and means to do so. Universities are unique places where lecturers try to disseminate open-ended knowledge in a free environment. There are clubs and societies – social, political, religious and others. Muslim students can form Islamic Societies in which they have the opportunity to get involved in a variety of activities. They should also be actively involved in students' union activities so that they can enhance their creative qualities for the benefit of all in society. However, it is important for young Muslims to maintain the right balance between their Islamic, social and academic activities in order to prepare themselves for a greater role later on in society.

Higher education provides the opportunity to gain skills in public relations, media relations, research and development, public outreach, government relations, and in defending civil and legal rights. It also facilitates young people to embark on the physical and biological sciences that are a part of the foundation of modern societies. As the future of the *ummah*, young Muslims must equip themselves with the practical knowledge relevant to bringing about positive changes in society for the common good.

Unfortunately, in an atmosphere of ignorance about Islam, some Muslim youth may be tempted to conceal their Muslim identity. This comes from their lack of knowledge and self-respect in the midst of the negative media image of Muslims today. However, it is vital that young Muslims in university feel proud to be who they are. Islam is a gift, not something to be embarrassed about or arrogant with. It is comprehensive divine guidance delivered by the last Prophet, Muhammad ﷺ, and the Qur'an has remained free from human adulteration. Muslims built dazzling and humane civilisations that enabled diverse human beings to live and prosper in harmony for over a thousand years. Muslim civilisation was the home of pre-eminent scientists and intellectual thinkers who were instrumental in expanding the frontiers of knowledge, which in turn was instrumental in ushering in the European Renaissance.

Universities are places of innovation, creativity and radical ideas. As in wider society they can breed extremist groups and ideas. In a polarised world today, Muslim students should be on their guard and steer clear of anything which goes beyond the well-defined path of moderation shown by the Qur'an and *Sunnah*.

Da'wah Opportunities

Da'wah means inviting people to Islam's message of loyalty to Allah, not proselytisation. Muslim youth should be proud, though not arrogant, with the knowledge and understanding that Allah has gifted them with. It is an Islamic duty to 'enjoin good and forbid evil' (Surah Ali Imran 3:104). Young Muslims with their creative ideas can truly help themselves and others by engaging in society to discuss how they can collectively work for the common good of all. Everything that a Muslim does, says, wears, eats or spends time doing should carry a positive message. Our personal appearance with, say, dress, beard and *hijab*, and our character with humility and positive behaviour as well as hard work are all important signposts of who we are. Everything that we do in our daily lives bears the testimony of Islam and can attract people to or drive them away from Islam.

Islam demands transparency in action and integrity of character. We should be confident enough to explain why we cannot go to the bar or pub to socialise, without us resenting those who do this. People make choices in their lives and all human beings are different. We should be honest if we are going to pray in our lunch hour. We should keep our promises and honour our word. We should not backbite or reveal the faults of others. This open practice encourages and emboldens fellow Muslims. It also evokes curiosity about and interest in Islam in other people's minds. Many converts to Islam have said that humility and simple actions of individual Muslims were instrumental for their conversion, not any overt effort by Muslims.

Islam and Khidmah (serving or helping others)

A revert Muslim called Emma (not her real name) once mentioned how she came to Islam. In her university years she was sharing a flat with a Muslim student, Fahmida (again not her real name). Fahmida was a practising Muslim and she was very sociable and soft in manner. Emma and Fahmida became good friends. They used to discuss many things, including religion. However, they never crossed the limit of each other's personal space or interfered in sensitive areas of the other's life. Fahmida was more careful in this. However, the thing that slightly irritated Emma in the beginning was Fahmida's stealthy prayer in the early hours of the morning. But Emma gradually got used to it. Fahmida herself expressed apology for this inconvenience she was causing to Emma. As time passed, Fahmida's humility and considerate nature drew her closer to Emma.

On one occasion Emma fell ill and it took her longer than expected to recover. Being away from the family she felt really vulnerable during that period. But, Fahmida, with her real *khidmah* character, attended to her friend like a nurse. Emma felt that Fahmida was not only trying to help her friend, she had an innate love and care for Emma. She was overwhelmed, and thanked Fahmida for all that she had done. She now recalls – it opened her eyes for Islam. But she did not realise it at that time. They parted when they finished their degree. But it was not easy for Emma to forget Fahmida. They kept in touch with each other and exchanged gifts on important occasions.

Unfortunately, within a few years Emma lost contact with Fahmida, as both of them changed their jobs. However, Emma had always Fahmida's smiley face in her mind. Under the pressure of work she once again fell ill, this time seriously so. Lying in bed, she could only remember Fahmida. But this time she was all alone. In lonely periods of reflection she often conjured up Fahmida's serene and happy face. She rebuked herself as to why she lost contact with Fahmida. She did not realise that, by attaching herself so closely to Fahmida, she was coming closer to Islam.

After a long period of convalescence, Emma went to the local library, as she always used to do. This time she was looking for books on religion, especially Islam. When she saw a translation of the Qur'an she immediately remembered that Fahmida used to read this book with deep devotion. Fahmida once mentioned that the Qur'an is the healing of all diseases of the heart and contains the solution to all human problems. Emma borrowed the translation and read it within a month. The following month she ended up in a local mosque and accepted Islam.

The Cycle of Life

As adolescents become adults, they take on board the role their parents took or should have taken. At this time, it may become apparent that some parents have failed in their responsibilities or could not quite make it in their roles as parents. The new generation should not waste time blaming their predecessors. They have an Islamic obligation to respect their parents and make up for their weaknesses tactfully.

Muslims are never complacent, even for a single moment. We attempt to improve upon our shortcomings and that continues unabated until our last breath. All parents have a stake in their children. To Muslim parents, time is important and, as such, every moment has to be productive, whether that involves a moment of deep reflection on the meaning of our existence, a moment in prayer or remembrance of Allah, those moments given to earning a livelihood, or those spent with one's family and people around us. We may not achieve immediate or tangible results in what we do, but we know our actions are being continuously recorded by the 'Noble Recorders' (Surah al-Infitar 82:11). The Prophet Muhammad ﷺ said,

> He whose two days are equal (in accomplishments) is a sure loser. (Sunan ad-Daylami)

Has Parenting Been Successful?

Success in parenting comes about when children grow with their natural qualities into responsible adults. Muslim adults have a responsibility not only towards themselves, their families and community, but also towards the *ummah* and humanity at large. Parents who dedicate their efforts to educating their children and creating in them a wider vision of humanity are blessed with Allah's favours.

Guiding young people to become self-respecting and self-motivating human beings in modern times is definitely a major challenge. In the world of apathy, and often hostility, towards religion and craving for self-gratification and egocentrism, communal feelings or working together for a common purpose are generally missing, but the success of Islam lies in the unity of the *ummah* and we are commanded to 'hold fast to the rope of Allah all together, and do not separate' (Surah Ali Imran 3:103). Parents should be instrumental in bringing their children to feel sympathy and work for the community on the one hand and the good of the society on the other. When we ourselves are actively involved in such works, our children will naturally follow suit.

The Muslim *ummah* is now large in numbers, but what is their impact in the international community? How many Muslims were there in the beginning when they ventured to shape the world in the mould of Islam? While quantity is important in itself, Islam's strength was always derived from the quality of its adherents. What is most needed today are Muslims who possess vision, passion and action to transform the *ummah* once again to be the 'best nation' on earth. Humanity today needs the type of Muslims - those who have voluntarily surrendered to Allah - who have the sense of urgency and commitment to re-establish a society that follows the spirit of Islam and love for humanity; a society based on shared values such as love, tolerance, respect, fairness and justice.

There is a worry of increased levels of hostility towards Islam and Muslims in many parts of the world today, due to political factors and the un-Islamic conduct of a tiny minority of Muslims themselves. But it is also true that after centuries of stagnation and disunity there are evidently attempts within Muslim communities to improve themselves. Muslims are going through a long period of soul searching and there are good signs of positive development in many areas.

On the other hand, in spite of material prosperity and colossal technological progress, the modern world is now undergoing a period of challenging political and economic crisis with massive social consequences. The balance of power is gradually and steadily shifting away from the West and nobody knows how the world will be in a generation's time. Inequality within communities and among people or nations has risen significantly, violation of human rights and civil liberty in many parts of the world is becoming a growing concern and social unrest is on the rise. It is a testing time for all of us. Conscientious young Muslims should be watching this with interest and work with young people in the wider society to make sure our world does not give in to the forces of intolerance and hate.

Chapter Seven

Conclusion

Correct action is a gift from Allah, but adab comes from the parents. (Al-Adab al-Mufrad al-Bukhari)

Children undergo radical physical as well as emotional changes when they enter into adolescence. Parents must therefore adopt a similarly enhanced approach to dealing with their offspring at this stage. While young children have greater physical and emotional demands and need care and protection, young adults need emotional support, guidance, empathy and understanding so that they can blossom into the best human beings that they can possibly be. In order to do this, parents must adopt a more accommodating and flexible approach bearing in mind that there will have to be negotiation and compromise along the way on both sides.

Adolescents are at the threshold of a very turbulent phase in their life. In addition to the changes in their body, they are gaining a new understanding of the world around them and are trying to carve out a role for themselves within it. For some, this is an exciting challenge that is embraced wholeheartedly, while others are scared of the unknown and feel insecure. Many teenagers will swing between both feelings during this phase and the result is a young person with contrasting characters – enthusiastic and animated one minute and sulky and uncooperative the next.

Parents who are aware or forewarned of these changes, do not feel daunted and are armed with the techniques to handle them will find that the teenage years will pass smoothly and end in a closer relationship between parent and child. The most important aspect to parenting is to provide a wholesome home environment for children filled with the bliss of spirituality, unconditional love and respect for family members and accommodation in wider society. When children's foundations are laid in such an environment they grow to be emotionally, spiritually and socially balanced human beings that are an asset to their parents and community. They are then, in turn, able to make a positive contribution to society at large.

This is easier said than done. Parents must be aware of their own actions, words and deeds and seek to emulate the best of human beings in all that they say and do, the Prophet Muhammad ﷺ. Parents must try to live their own lives with the universal values of kindness, good speech, honesty, modesty, integrity and strive to always be of service to others. Just as a good tree will bear good fruit, parents of good moral character will find this reflected in their children.

A significant ingredient to achieve this is to spend time with children; this quality time where the parent is available without any distraction is vital for the parent-child relationship. Children need to know that their parents are there for them, available to talk, to listen, to offer advice or maybe just for a pat or hug. An open and communicative relationship between parents and children can often reveal potential challenges children may go through at an early stage.

Teenagers will have ups and downs in their life and may go through mood swings and erratic changes. Parents can help by providing a stable and reassuring surrounding for them. It is tempting for parents to shout at a teenager when they are behaving badly or acting up. The parental skills of stress control and anger management are vital if they are to show their children the model way to behave. Often a child who 'acts out' may have hidden fears and insecurities. So, reassure them that they are loved and, difficult as it may be, invite them to talk about it. Children may not always do what their parents wish. They will keep on making mistakes. Conscientious parents know when to leave their teenagers alone to reflect upon their actions and when to step in and apply some sensible disciplinary intervention. Traditional domineering strategies of discipline and control are almost always counterproductive and most teenagers will rebel against an authority that is seen to be inhibiting their creativity and inquisitiveness. However, sensible teenagers also know that it is in their own best interest to seek advice and guidance from their parents. Teenagers can learn enormously from their parents' greater experience and wider world view.

Parents must not pretend to be perfect in raising their children and working with their adolescents. Most young people do realise the constraints of their parents; what they expect from their parents is empathy and understanding for their new journey in life. Any growth in itself has its pains. The transfer from childhood to adult life for Muslim children in Western countries brings with it a number of issues. An awareness of these issues and an understanding of their impact on a young person's life are vital if parents are to guide their children through the uncertain maze of life.

The surrounding materialistic and hedonistic culture is presented to young people through the media as glamorous. No wonder they are charmed and sometimes hypnotised by it. The reality is that society is experiencing a real challenge on its values, ethos and character. Post-modern societies are becoming increasingly selfish and exclusive rather than caring and inclusive. Our young people are thrown into the deep end of consumerism and as a result they often lose focus of life's higher meaning. Many suffer from an identity crisis, inferiority complex and confusion. The result is a significant number of our youth who have deviated from 'the middle path' of Islam – either by abandoning its principles altogether or by taking them to an extreme.

Poor parenting is one of the root causes of almost all of the problems that we are experiencing with our youth today and it is a major barrier to the progress of our diverse communities. Parents who fail to invest their time and efforts into parenting when necessary will see the unpleasant fruits in their old age. But it will be too late then. Not only will they be losers in this world but most probably also in the Hereafter.

Positive parenting is an obligation for us and it is linked with the purpose of our life on earth. It is vital for our *Dunya* and *Akhirah*. The purpose of parenting is to develop effective stewardship on earth through love and care on the one hand and proper education and training on the other. Effective parenting means passing on values, ethos and a sense of responsibility to children when they grow as adolescents and adults. A well-disciplined and stable family environment anchors adolescents with their parents, family and the community. Through this they earn a sense of belonging to their own community and learn how to relate to wider society. They also learn how to love our nature and its ecological balance as true stewards on earth are supposed to do. The legacy of good parenting lasts for generations and the result is a community that lives up to its title of being 'the best nation on earth'.

Our community and *ummah* today need dynamic and inspirational people with *Sahabah*-type features and qualities, who with their vision, passion and action will be the catalysts for a rejuvenated society for the good of all. Recreation of this new generation of youth - deep in their knowledge of Islam and contemporary society, balanced in their action and love for humanity - is a historic task for Muslim parents. Individual families need to mobilise their full potential with a view to training, educating, and leading their adolescents so that when they grow as adults they can defend the dignity of their religion and community from fanatical extremism on the one hand and Islamophobic bigotry on the other.

Our individual life is short and the task on us is huge. Islam has taught Muslims to prioritise between compulsory, preferred and recommended acts when it comes to religious rituals. The spirit of Islam demands from us similar priorities in our personal, professional, family and social life. This is according to the *Sunnah* of Prophet Muhammad ﷺ. Positive parenting is thus the most important priority, especially in the present challenges of post-modern society.

It will be a tragedy if Muslim parents fail to help their adolescents in their journey of life in the West. It will be a shame if our young Muslims have to compromise with their religion to live in a pluralist society where Muslim culture has the potential to flourish. I am in no way saying the job of parenting is easy, what I am saying is it is perfectly possible. It is also a test and trust from Allah. At the end of the day, success comes from Allah and He only bestows guidance on those who have patience (*sabr*), gratefulness (*shukr*), reliance on Him (*tawakkul*) and who repent for their shortcomings and weaknesses (*tawba*).

One final word: In this exhilarating journey that has its ups and downs, we must not forget to actually enjoy the company of our children. Young people are inherently innocent, instinctively happy and ever creative and adventurous. Their company transmits liveliness and innocence and brings a fresh perspective to us elders, who are sometimes overburdened with the affairs of the world. Parenting, if it is understood and creatively done, is a joy and an adventure.